LET GOD'S
LIGHT SHINE
FORTH

LET GOD'S LIGHT SHINE FORTH

The Spiritual Vision of
POPE BENEDICT XVI

EDITED AND WITH AN INTRODUCTION BY
ROBERT MOYNIHAN

IMAGE BOOKS
DOUBLEDAY
New York London Toronto Sydney Auckland

AN IMAGE BOOK
PUBLISHED BY DOUBLEDAY

A hardcover edition of this book was originally
published in 2005 by Doubleday.

Published in the United States by Doubleday, an
imprint of The Doubleday Broadway Publishing Group,
a division of Random House, Inc., New York.
www.doubleday.com

IMAGE, DOUBLEDAY, and the portrayal of a deer
drinking from a stream are registered
trademarks of Random House, Inc.

Book design by Michael Collica

Library of Congress Cataloging-in-Publication Data is
on file with the Library of Congress.

ISBN-13: 978-0-385-50793-6
ISBN-10: 0-385-50793-3

PRINTED IN THE UNITED STATES OF AMERICA

1 3 5 7 9 8 6 4 2

First Paperback Edition

To my parents,
Ruth and William T. Moynihan

CONTENTS

Part One: The Man and His Life
by Robert Moynihan

1

Part Two: The Spiritual Vision of Benedict XVI

77

THE CHRISTIAN PILGRIM

Part Three: The Pontificate of Benedict XVI

177

Part One

THE MAN AND HIS LIFE

Robert Moynihan

"We are supposed to be the light of the world, and that means that we should allow the Lord to be seen through us. We do not wish to be seen ourselves, but wish for the Lord to be seen through us. It seems to me that this is the real meaning of the Gospel when it says 'act in such a way that people who see you may see the work of God and praise God.' Not that people may see the Christians but 'by means of you, God.' Therefore, the person must not appear, but allow God to be seen through his person."

—*Pope Benedict XVI,*
conversation with Robert Moynihan, February 23, 1993

"The Presence of God"

On April 19, 2005, in Rome, Joseph Cardinal Ratzinger, at age 78, was chosen by the cardinals of the Roman Catholic Church to be the 265th successor of the apostle Peter, bishop of Rome and head of the universal Church. The world was genuinely astonished. Why? In large measure, because they were surprised that a group of cardinals representing places like Argentina, Nigeria, and India had not chosen a younger, more "progressive" cardinal from the Third World to "reform" and "modernize" traditional Christian doctrines and emphasize issues of social justice. Instead, they had chosen an elderly German cardinal, Joseph Ratzinger, who, over the previous quarter century as head of the Vatican's chief doctrinal office (the Congregation for the Doctrine of the Faith), had earned a reputation for defending the traditional teachings of the Church and for emphasizing the priority of the "right worship" of God in any effort to build a just human society.

How did this happen? Why did it happen? What does it mean?

Over the past 30 years, not only the cardinals who elected Ratzinger as Pope, but many Catholics, and other men and women of good will around the world, have come to agree with Benedict that the greatest "crisis" facing the Church and the world is "the absence of God"—a culture and way of life without any transcendent dimension, without any orientation toward eternity, toward the sacred, toward the divine. And that the "solution" to this "crisis" is quite simple to express in a phrase: the world needs "the presence of God."

Benedict had long argued that the "absence of God" in the modern world, the "secularization" of modern "globalized" society, has created a society in which the human person no longer has any sure protection against the depredations of power or, more importantly, any clear understanding of the meaning and ultimate destination of his life.

Yet his call to reorient human culture toward God has never meant an abandonment of the search for social justice. Rather, it has always been a challenge to place that search within the Christian context of repentance and belief in the Gospel.

Benedict's focus on the "priority" of knowing and loving God before doing anything else whatsoever was seen by the vast majority of the college of cardinals as the right focus.

Benedict was elected by his fellow cardinals, including many from very poor countries, because they agreed with him about the need for a Pope who could preach the priority of God, and in so doing, lay the only secure foundation for a just society.

In understanding the vision of Benedict XVI, we begin not by examining his many theological works formulated over the past 50 years, but by listening as he himself describes his own beginning. His words, based on several interviews from 1993 to 1995 and also on his autobiography (published in 1998 as *Milestones: Memoirs 1927–1977*), reveal a man who sees the world and everyday life with a sense of wonder, as if all things are crisscrossed with hints or "traces" of God.

Indeed, this is ultimately Benedict's great message: that the world is a sacrament—an "outward sign" of the "inward reality" of God's love, and that man will only be happy when he recognizes the primacy of God in his own life and in the entire world.

Benedict's conviction that creation is joyful insofar as it is oriented toward God began in his childhood in Bavaria, where Catholicism and everyday life were interwoven. The root of that conviction is seen in his early and deep appreciation for the liturgy, the ritual celebration of the Christian mysteries using the symbolism of everyday life—water, wine, bread, light and darkness.

It is evident in his love for the simple life of the Bavarian countryside, which he speaks of fondly as one of the happiest periods of his life; in his appreciation for the simple men and women of faith; in his rejection of Nazis, whose inhumane violence he saw as the fruit of their ideological rejection of God; in his later life, when as a theological advisor at the Second Vatican Council his desire to make the wonder of God more accessible and visible to more people earned him a reputation as a "progressive"; in his 25 years as Prefect of the Church's doctrinal office, where he labored to protect the wonder and beauty of God from being encrusted and hidden under theologies of relativism, atheist Marxism, and secularism.

Ultimately it is evident in his first homilies as Pope Benedict XVI, as he called on all men and women, both in and out of the Church, to "seek God's face," traveling along with him on the journey that leads to an eternal home, where God is entirely present, and so true joy is everlasting.

From Marktl to Freising

"My earliest memory really goes back to Marktl, and this is the only memory I have of this earliest period in my life. I must have been just two years old, because we moved away from Marktl when I was two. In our house we were on the second floor, and on the ground floor there was a dentist, and this person had a motor car—something that was still rather rare at that time, at least in Bavaria. And the smell of the gasoline from this car is what I remember." With a laugh, he added, "I was deeply impressed by that."

Pope Benedict XVI was born on April 16, 1927, in the little town of Marktl am Inn, in the Bavarian diocese of Passau, in southern Germany. He was born as the third child of Joseph and Maria Ratzinger, after siblings Georg and Maria.

In that year, April 16 fell on Holy Saturday, the "silent time" in the Christian liturgy between the sorrow of Good Friday and the joy of Easter Sunday.

"I was baptized on the morning after my birth with water just blessed during the Easter vigil. My family often remarked on this; being the first baby to be baptized with this new water was an important sign."

One senses the underlying "genetic code" of Benedict's spiritual life in this intimate union of everyday life and the life of faith: his birth precedes his baptism by only a few hours; his family is always present, reminding him during his childhood that he was the first to be baptized in the new holy water, inculcating in him the sense of his dignity and uniqueness—a chief task of all parents, brothers and sisters; and his faith, woven into the fabric of everyday life. "The faith penetrated all of life, though not everyone was a serious, believing Catholic. In the countryside and small towns, no one yet could, or even wished, to step outside the fabric of Catholic life, of Christian life."

Faith and family have remained the twin poles of Benedict's consciousness throughout his life. First, family: his memoirs show him always eager to return to his parents' house, to go on long walks with his mother and father, to live "in family" or "as a family" as often and as long as possible. Indeed, his parents would come to live with him when he took his first university teaching job. "I always remember, with great affection, the goodness of my father and mother." His sister, Maria, who never married, would become his housekeeper, keeping the Ratzinger family together even in Rome, until her death—which was devastating for Benedict—in November 1991. Benedict also spends much of his summer vacation in the company of his brother, Georg, a priest who is a musicologist and the director of the cathedral choir in Regensburg, Germany.

Then the other pole: faith. "I have always been grateful for the fact that my life was from the very beginning immersed in the Paschal mystery, since it could not be seen as anything but a sign of benediction. Of course, my birth was not on Easter Sunday, but Holy Saturday. And yet, the more I reflect, the more it seems characteristic of our human existence, which still awaits Easter, is still not in full light, but confidently sets out toward the light."

The simplicity of these words reveals a key point in Benedict's thinking: that the faith of the simple, common people is often the purist kind.

Not far from Marktl am Inn, where he was born, is the Marian sanctuary of Altoetting, which dates back to Carolingian times (the ninth century). When Benedict was a boy, the simple friar Conrad of Parzham, who had been a doorman at the sanctuary, was beatified. "In this man, humble and kind, we saw incarnated the best of our people, led by the faith to realize its very highest possibilities. Later, I would often reflect on this extraordinary circumstance, that the Church, in the century of progress and of faith in science, saw herself best represented precisely by the most simple persons, like Bernadette of Lourdes or Brother Conrad."

The annual cycle of worship in prayer, which, in the Catholic Church, is called the "liturgical year," also made a deep impression on young Benedict. As the seasons changed from winter to spring to summer to fall, so the Church festivals changed, from Lent to Easter to Pentecost to Christmas, providing everyday life with a different, deeper dimension. "The liturgical year gave to time its rhythm, and

I perceived this fact from the time I was an infant, yes, from the time I was an infant, with great joy."

For Christmas, the family manger scene grew larger each year, and the sometimes gray and melancholy days of German winter were brightened by the Advent liturgies: "They were celebrated at dawn, the church still dark, illuminated only by candles."

His recollection of his childhood Easters reveals the extent to which Benedict's faith sprang out of a rich fabric of Christian symbolism, still almost "baroque" in comparison with post–Vatican II liturgy introduced in the 1960s: "For all of Holy Week, the windows of the church were covered by black coverings. Even in daytime, the church was shrouded in a darkness dense with mystery. But the instant the parish priest sang out the verse that announced 'He is Risen!' the coverings were suddenly pulled back from the windows and a radiant light flooded into the entire church: it was the most impressive representation of the resurrection of Christ I can imagine."

Life was peaceful in Marktl, and in the other area towns where the family lived during the 1930s. His father was a police officer and his mother "an excellent cook."

"My mother was a professional cook before she married," he said, smiling at the recollection. "In the last years before she was married she worked in a hotel in Munich where the cooks each had an area of specialization. She was a specialist in *mehlspeiss*. Do you know what that is? It is something that exists only in Austria and Bavaria. They are pastries made with flour and cream, not like the Italian pasta, but sweet. *Apfel strudel* and things like that. *Apfel strudel* is the only item that has spread more or less around the world, but we have many choices of this type. An extraordinary abundance! And we loved these *mehlspeissen* very much. Beyond that, we were, of course, quite poor, and she had to do what she could to feed a family of five people. Usually we ate a little beef, some salad, vegetables . . .

"I lived in a small town with people who work in agriculture and handicrafts, and there I feel most at home."

With the coming of Nazism, German attitudes toward the Church's role in everyday life began to change. "The fanatics, naturally, left the Church and openly opposed the Church." But not everyone became a Nazi. Indeed, many did not. "I would say, those fanatics who explicitly declared that they were anti-Catholic, anti-Christian, were, in the rural areas, quite few. Many people were, as we say in German, *'mitlaufer'* ("going along"), no? People who did what was necessary without being very committed personally, and at the same time continued to go to Church, continued to take part in this religious life which was so much a part of the everyday fabric of rural German life at the time, so much so that it was unimaginable that one would not take part.

"But there was also a committed Catholic group that lived a committed Catholic life. And, just as the fanatics were a minority, so too were the members of this group. They were deeply committed Christians, and so were profoundly opposed to the regime."

The family moved to Tittmunning, then to Aschau, then to Traunstein, a little city in the foothills of the Alps. These relocations were directly related to young Benedict's father's resistance to Nazism, which resulted in demotions and transfers in his work as a police officer. "Our father was a bitter enemy of Nazism because he believed it was in conflict with our faith," the Pope's brother, Georg, has said.

"Tittmunning was a lovely little town with a certain history, because it belonged to the archdiocese of Salzburg. A beautiful town. Even in the 1500s, it was the point of departure for a movement of Church reform, a reform of the clergy. And the effects could be felt down even to our century, because the reform had established the common life of the clergy, and this remained the practice in that region, that the parish priests and assistant parish priests lived a common life.

"It was a very small town, only 3,000 inhabitants, but very lovely. And here I have some very clear memories, both of Church life and of nature, but especially of Church life. There were two large, beautiful churches. The parish church had a chapter and in the other church, which had belonged to the Augustinian canons, there were nuns. And in both churches there was lovely music, the churches were very beautiful . . . but my most vivid memories were the celebrations of Christmas and Holy Week.

"There was the tomb of Jesus there, from Holy Thursday to Holy Saturday, a beautiful baroque construction with many flowers and lights. And the sight of the holy tomb, the holy sepulcher, I should say, this deeply impressed me as a young child. Also other feasts, and Vespers with sacred chant. Processions. Every Thursday there was a great sung Mass and a procession with the Most Holy Sacrament. And in this way the beauty of the Church remained deeply ingrained in my memory. And Christmas, too, both at church, and at home, naturally, was also very beautiful."

The family lived in Tittmunning from 1929 to 1932. "We took long walks with my mother, in Austria, especially, because we were right on the Austrian border. The river which ran through the town formed the frontier between Germany and Austria."

Laughing, Benedict remembered that "there was a station, a little train which connected this little town with the rest of the world. But we, being poor, we never left from the city. We always went by foot to the first station, and always came back by foot from the first station. In this way, we saved a little money. These were wonderful walks. When I was only three, my mother sometimes carried me, but by the time I was four I could manage quite well on my own.

"Naturally, we did not have many books in our house but my father had a great interest in history and also in politics, and my mother in novels, and so there were quite a few books of history, and also religious books, naturally, and then also quite a few novels, like *Ben Hur* and *Quo Vadis*, and others."

Though Joseph's father was chief of police, he came from a traditional family of farmers from lower Bavaria. "My father, even if he had little formal education, was a person who, intellectually speaking, was absolutely superior, of great superiority even in comparison with academics. He had his convictions, which he deepened through study, of course. He was a great Bavarian patriot. That is, he did not willingly accept Bismarck's empire and the incorporation of Bavaria into Prussianized Germany. And one must say that there were always, or for some time, these two currents in Bavaria: one reconciled with this idea of a unified Germany, and the other that did not accept this idea and thought rather in the context of ancient history, back before the French Revolution. They identified with the Holy Roman Empire, that is, with the ideals of friendship or close relations with Austria, and also with France. And my father was oriented this way, and he was above all a committed

Catholic, and therefore he had a position which was very clear against nationalism. His arguments were so well founded that he simply convinced us."

Nazism and War

Hitler took power when Benedict was six years old. The National Socialist regime at first had little evident impact on life in Bavaria, Ratzinger recalls, but a local teacher was enthusiastic about Nazi ideology. "With great pomp, he caused a May tree to be raised and composed a sort of prayer to the symbol of the ever-renewed life force. That tree was intended to represent the beginning of the restoration of the Germanic religion, contributing to the repression of Christianity, denounced as an element alienating people from their great Germanic culture. With the same intention, he organized a summer solstice festival, again as a return to the sacrality of nature, and in polemic with the ideas of sin and redemption, which were said to have been imposed on us by the alien religion of Jews and Romans.

"When my father was transferred to Tittmunning, he was above all thinking of the better schools a larger town could provide. But then came the time of the depression and mass unemployment. It was the period from 1929 to 1932, this great economic crisis in the world. And so there was enormous unemployment. And this unemployment favored the growth of National Socialism. These unemployed men hoped Hitler could change something. And on this point he did change something, by creating an army, and so forth. It was a strong movement, and also aggressive.

"My father came out strongly against the Nazi movement, and when he saw that it was no longer avoidable that

Hitler would come to power, he transferred to another small town, Aschau, because there, at Tittmunning, at the moment when Hitler came to power, it would certainly have been very difficult for the family. He left at the right moment, one month before this change, to the small town of Aschau where, naturally, these changes were also visible but they did not have such an impact on daily life due to the agricultural lifestyle. So here one could survive, even if there were always pressures, always difficulties."

In 1933, the year Hitler was made Chancellor of Germany, Joseph had started school and was beginning to experience the impact of the Nazi regime. "The Party had installed Nazis among the teachers at the school, and also my father's deputy police chief was a young fervent Nazi. These realities were present." But "everyday life, even in school, I would say, was not deeply penetrated by these phenomena. We were rather distant from the evolution of political events. One heard some things about it. But it was more difficult for my father because there were continual, let us say, insinuations from above to do something against the parish priest, or other priests who came, and nuns. There were always many difficulties.

"My father knew that they no longer gave the orders to him but directly to his second-in-command. But he would know about the orders, and so he would go to the parish priest or other priests and say to them: 'Look, this is going to happen or that is going to happen.' And so he could help. One time, but I do not know the details, it had already been decided to imprison a certain priest, but my father was able, at the right moment, to warn the priest. He carried out some maneuver, I don't know what, and was able to save him.

"I had already begun to attend school. It was 1934 when Hitler decided to execute some of the SA leaders.* Our teacher spoke to us about these things, about the 'night of the long knives.' She said: 'These men wanted to do bad things and the Fuhrer became aware of that and has protected us against them.' I don't know how the people interpreted it. When Hitler did something, my father was always suspicious that he intended evil. Because, my father said, and this was one of his sayings—'Nothing good ever comes from the devil, even if it seems to be so.' But if he was really aware that the suppression of the SA was actually a trick to display himself as the Fuhrer of all the Germans, this I don't know.

"In those towns in the 1930s, in the rural areas, everything was almost peaceful. The people had their rhythm of life and little changed. But I would say that one could see that Hitler was preparing a war. My father said that from the beginning: 'Now we have this scoundrel, and soon we'll be at war.' One could perceive that war was coming. But . . . during the first four years, in the atmosphere of daily life, there was no real thought of this. The situation changed at the moment of the annexation of Austria. We then lived in Traunstein, not far from the frontier, and we could sense the great tension. From that moment it was clear that things were not going well."

In 1937, Joseph's father had retired and the family moved to Traunstein. "Things were rougher in Traunstein, but here the worst incidents had taken place before our arrival. Here

---

* The storm troopers led by Ernst Röhm who helped Hitler to power, but who were suppressed by him out of fear that they might turn against him.

they had broken the teeth of one priest, and a number of incidents of this type. They had put a bomb in the residence of the canons which exploded and damaged the parish house. And the cardinal had penalized the city with an interdict: the bells of the city could no longer be rung. Mass was still celebrated, but for a city which loved music and was steeped in the musical tradition of Salzburg, it was a severe punishment."

As a child, Benedict never personally experienced any physical threats or violence at the hands of the oppressive regime.

In the late 1930s, at the insistence of the local parish priest, he entered a minor seminary. "For two years I had walked back and forth to school each day with great joy; but now the parish priest insisted I enter the minor seminary. At Easter in 1939 [Ratzinger was just 12], I entered the seminary." His brother was already there, and he knew many of his classmates, but he hated the strict, confining regimen. "At home I had lived and studied in great freedom, as I wished, building my own little boyhood world. Now, compelled to study in a hall with 60 other boys, it was torture. It became almost impossible for me to study, whereas before it had been very easy."

Worst of all, each day the boys had two hours of sports. "This circumstance became a true torture for me, since I was not at all athletically inclined, and was the smallest of all the boys in the school, many of whom were three years older than I was. I was less physically strong than almost all of them by a large margin. My companions were quite tolerant, but, in the long run, it's no fun to have to live off of the tolerance of others and to know that one is only a burden to one's team."

Benedict had felt a calling to the priesthood from early childhood, so it seemed like a natural choice to him. "During those years, however, it was a bit of a fiction, because the seminary had been requisitioned as a military hospital for war wounded at the outset of the war. So I formally and juridically belonged to the seminary, but in fact, because the seminary was a military hospital, I lived at home. But since I was legally a member of the seminary, when the seminary as such was taken and transferred to Munich to assist in this antiaircraft work, I also was forced to go."

In 1941 it became mandatory to join the Hitler Youth, and Joseph was forced to place his name on the rolls. "As a seminarian, I was registered in the Hitler Youth. As soon as I was out of the seminary, I never went back. And that was difficult, because the tuition reduction, which I really needed, was tied to proof of attendance at Hitler Youth meetings. Thank goodness, there was a very understanding mathematics teacher. He himself was a Nazi but an honest man, who said to me, 'Just go once and get the document so that we have it.' When he saw that I simply didn't want to, he said, 'I understand, I'll take care of it,' and so I was able to stay free of it."

The war came. "At the beginning the war seemed almost unreal." There was the sudden conquest of Poland in September 1939, then the quiet winter of 1939–40, then the triumph of the Nazis over France in the spring and summer of 1940. "Even those who opposed National Socialism felt a sort of patriotic satisfaction," Benedict recalls. "Hubert Jedin, the great historian of the Councils, later my colleague at Bonn, had to leave Germany because he was of Jewish origin. He passed the war years in involuntary exile in the Vatican. In his memoirs, he has described with penetrating words the strange conflict of emotions that the events of that year produced in him."

But Benedict's father saw clearly. "My father saw with unalterable clarity that the victory of Hitler would not be a victory for Germany, but for Antichrist, and would be the beginning of apocalyptic times for all believers, and not only for them."

Then came the attack on Russia on June 22, 1941. "I will never forget the sunny Sunday in 1941 when the news came that Germany and its allies had launched an attack on the Soviet Union along a front from Cape North to the Black Sea. That day my class had met for a boat trip on a nearby lake. The trip was lovely, but the news of the widening of the war loomed over us like a nightmare and paralyzed our joy. This time things couldn't go well. We thought of Napoleon; we thought of the vast, endless plains of Russia, where the German assault would be consumed."

Within a few months, the lines of war wounded were returning. The seminary building was requisitioned as a hospital. Benedict went to his parents' home.

In 1943, at age 16, not yet old enough for true military service, he was called up to serve as an auxiliary in a German antiaircraft unit, and so became a member of the German Army.

"It was something I could not escape. And those who lived in a monastery and seminary and, therefore, were already in a common life and outside of the home, had to go, as a community, to join this antiaircraft artillery.

"The situation was quite strange. It was not simply military service, because our schooling continued. In the morning, the professors came from Munich and we had lessons. And in the afternoons as well, there were usually two hours dedicated to study. And there was also an order that the youth protection laws were valid also for us. That is, for example, we were forbidden to smoke." The authorities took several other measures "to guarantee the morality of these young men . . . as soldiers."

But the young seminarians all knew that they were not welcome in Hitler's Germany. "We certainly wanted the defeat of Nazism, there was no doubt about that. One thing was clear: the Nazis wanted, after the war, to eliminate the Church. There would definitely be no more priests. This was one reason we longed for their defeat.

"We did not do very much that was concrete because we were primarily for technical services, radar, that type of thing. We learned how to fire a rifle, but only as an exercise. Three stages existed in the army, which I had to undergo. First, we were assistants for the antiaircraft artillery and, as I said, it was a time with a 'mixed' character, since we were both a community studying and, at the same time, doing our military service. Once, for a lesson, we even went to Munich in order to use the physics and chemistry equipment there. And the community in itself was interesting. Not without tensions, naturally. But there was a sense of mutual help. And there was the military service. But it was not an all-consuming activity. This lasted until September 1944."

On September 10, 1944, now 17, he was released from that duty and went home. There he found a notice that he had been drafted into a work unit to dig trenches on the Austrian front.

"In September 1944, we were released and transferred to the so-called 'work service,' a service that Hitler had established in 1933 in order to create work; we entered this service, and were sent to the frontier with Austria. And we had to learn how to work with picks and shovels, dig ditches, that type of thing. So we were on the Austrian frontier at the moment of the capitulation of Hungary to the Russians. At that moment we began to work to create impediments against the Red Army. We dug great ditches to block tanks, for example.

"One night we were pulled out of our bunks and gathered together in our exercise fatigues, still half-asleep. An SS official called us out one by one from the line and sought to persuade us to enroll 'voluntarily' in the SS, exploiting our exhaustion and the position of each one of us before the whole group. Many, even some who were good fellows, were enrolled in this way into this criminal corps. Together with a few others, I had the fortune to be able to say that I intended to become a Catholic priest. We were covered with hisses and insults and kicked back inside, but we were grateful for these humiliations since they freed us from the threat of this false 'voluntary' enrollment with all its consequences.

"This service lasted two months.

"After that I became a true soldier, an infantryman. But, the official who assigned each person, these young people, was obviously against the war and against Nazism. He looked for the best places for us, and he said to me: 'You can go to the barracks of Traunstein,' where I would be at home. And so I was in the barracks at Traunstein, which was a little way outside the city, but not far from home. And here I had my training as a soldier, how to fire a gun and so forth. Finally, after two months, I became ill and was ill until the end of the war. It was nothing serious. I had suffered an injury to one of my hands. I hurt one of my thumbs while shooting in target practice. (He showed me the scar on his thumb.) In any case, the good Lord protected me."

Germany's armed forces slowly disintegrated, the Allied forces advanced and the war came to an end. Though he had never seen combat, Benedict was detained with tens of thousands of other German soldiers in a camp near Munich for several weeks. "We were in the open the entire time. Our food was a dish of soup and a piece of bread per day. When, after a long period of good weather, it began to rain, we formed little groups to try and find a bit of refuge from the bad weather."

This "war period" of Benedict's life changed his character and his worldview. "First, we became more aware of our faith, because we were often caught up in discussions, and we were obliged to find arguments to defend ourselves. And so in this sense, the challenges helped us to reflect on the faith, to lead a life more concrete and convinced of the faith.

"Second, we saw a certain anti-Christian vision of the world that, in the final analysis, showed itself to be anti-human and absurd, even though, when it came to power, it displayed itself as the great hope of humanity. As a result, I learned to have a certain reserve with regard to dominant ideologies."

Joseph was an American prisoner of war until June 19. "Then I was released and I returned home. Even the heavenly Jerusalem itself could not have appeared more beautiful to me at the moment I finally reached my home."

Priest, Professor, and Bishop (1951–1981)

"I could now dedicate myself completely . . . to preparing for the next big step: ordination to the priesthood . . . in 1951. At the solemn call on that radiant summer day, which I remember as the high point of my life, we re-

sponded *'Adsum,'* Here I am. We should not be supersti-
tious; but, at that moment when the elderly archbishop
laid his hands on me, a little bird—perhaps a lark—flew
up from the high altar in the cathedral and trilled a little
joyful song. And I could not but see in this a reassurance
from on high, as if I heard the words 'This is good, you
are on the right way.' "

—*Joseph Ratzinger,*
Milestones: Memoirs 1927–1977, *p. 99*

Benedict's personal life after the war was marked by
study, writing, teaching, and prayer. His great teacher was
St. Augustine (354–430), the supreme Church Father of the
Latin West, from whom all intellectual life in western culture for a thousand years descended, and whose influence
on our thought and view of the world even today is of profound importance.

Augustine in his *Confessions* reveals to us a human being
engaged in a soul-shattering struggle to win through, against
disordered passions and many sins, to faith in God and a
life of virtue.

Such struggles did not trouble Benedict's adolescence
and young manhood. He is in the blessed company of those
whose childhood faith grew organically into a lifelong
source of meaning and strength. He passed through no ti-
tanic spiritual struggle, no all-night wrestling, Jacob-like,
with the angel of the Lord, no "dark night" of doubt and
desolation, but rather matured, patiently and humbly, into
the faith imbued in him from his earliest days.

In this sense, his life story is a "modest" one, edifying
and admirable in a man who has arrived at such a height of
authority and responsibility. It is on the battlefield of the

mind, not the heart and passions, where Benedict engaged in spiritual combat.

After the war, together with his brother Georg, Benedict went on to study philosophy in Freising's seminary. In September 1947, he began his studies of theology in Munich's university, and concluded his courses in the summer of 1950.

Among his professors, one of his favorites was Friedrich Stummer, who taught Old Testament. "I attended his lectures and seminars with great interest," Ratzinger recalls. "In this way the Old Testament became important to me and I increasingly understood that the New Testament is not the book of another religion which had appropriated the Sacred Scriptures of the Jews as if they were, everything considered, of secondary importance. The New Testament is nothing other than an interpretation, starting from the story of Jesus, of 'laws, prophets, and writings' that at the time of Jesus had not yet reached their mature form in a definitive canon, but which were still open and therefore presented themselves to the disciples as evidence in favor of Christ, as Sacred Scriptures which revealed his mystery.

"I understood ever more clearly that Judaism (which in the strict sense begins with the conclusion of the process of formation of the scriptural canon and, therefore, in the first century after Christ) and the Christian faith, as it is described in the New Testament, are two ways to take possession of the Sacred Scriptures of Israel which depend finally on the position assumed with regard to the figure of Jesus of Nazareth. The Scripture, which we today call the Old Testament, is in itself open to both paths."

In the fall of 1949, Ratzinger was given a copy of Henri de Lubac's *Catholicism* by a friend. Reading de Lubac "transmitted to me a new and more profound relationship with the Fathers."

During 1950, Ratzinger prepared a dissertation on Augustine's theology of the Church, entering an area that would remain a central subject of his interest from that time forth. On June 26, 1951, he was ordained to priesthood by Cardinal Faulhaber in the Cathedral of Freising.

One month later he began his ministry as assistant pastor in the parish of the Precious Blood in Munich. His duties at the parish included teaching religious education, hearing confessions, taking care of the youth ministry, celebrating Masses, funerals, baptisms, and so on—riding everywhere on his bicycle. "Teaching 16 hours a week was a hefty bundle of work, especially when you're just beginning. I came to love it because I very quickly formed a good relationship with the children. It was quite a wonderful thing to translate the whole abstract (intellectual) concepts in such a way that they also said something to children."

For about 12 months he was a parish priest, but then he was called to be a seminary professor. It was the beginning of a quarter century of intense work in academic theology. In October 1952 he was assigned to the seminary in Freising. "On the one hand, this was the solution I had desired, the one that would enable me to return to my theological work, which I loved so much. On the other hand, I suffered a great deal from the loss of human contacts and experiences afforded me by the pastoral ministry. In fact, I even began to think I would have done better to remain in parish work. The feeling of being needed and of accomplishing an important service had helped me to give all I could, and this gave me a joy in the priesthood that I did not experience in so direct a manner in my new assignment."

Nine months later he received his doctorate in theology with a thesis entitled "The People and House of God in St. Augustine's Doctrine of the Church."

In the winter semester of 1954, he assumed the chair of dogmatic theology at the college of Freising. His family moved to Freising to assist him during his struggle in writing his postdoctoral thesis (called "Habilitationschrift" in German) while teaching.

Ratzinger gives us a fascinating glimpse into his academic difficulties in his account of the problems he faced in winning approval for his *Habilitationschrift*—the work required in Germany after the doctoral thesis in order to become a professor. The work was rejected the first time he handed it in, in the fall of 1955, a devastating blow to the young scholar. In addition to a dispute with a professor about the work's contents, the copy Ratzinger handed in on deadline was filled with typos; apparently his typist was incompetent and disorganized, losing sheets of the text and making it impossible for him to proofread his own work. Ratzinger cut about half the text and, to the faculty's astonishment, rewrote it in record time, winning approval for it in early 1957.

In 1959, the paths of Joseph and his brother Georg diverged. Georg took on the position of choir director in their home parish and Traunstein, and Joseph took on a professorship in Bonn. However, this experience was marred by the death of his father—after a stroke while Joseph was visiting him. "When I returned to Bonn after this experience, I sensed that the world was emptier for me and that a portion of my home had been transferred to the other world."

Over the following 5 years, Ratzinger made a reputation for himself in German theological circles. This put him in a position to become a *peritus*, or expert advisor, when the Second Vatican Council began in 1962. "Cardinal Frings took his secretary, Fr. Luthe, and me, as his theological advisors to Rome; he also saw to it that toward the end of the first session I received an official nomination as a theologian of the Council."

Joseph then went on to take up a lecturing post in Munster. But during 1963, his mother was diagnosed with stomach cancer. "Her goodness became even purer and more radiant and continued to shine unchanged even through the weeks of increasing pain. On the day after *Gaudete* Sunday, December 16, 1963, she closed her eyes forever, but the radiance of her goodness has remained, and for me it has become more and more a confirmation of the faith by which she had allowed herself to be formed. I know of no more convincing proof for the faith than precisely the pure and unalloyed humanity that the faith allowed to mature in my parents and in so many other persons I have had the privilege to encounter."

Benedict's years at the Council (each autumn from 1962–1965) were a "hinge-point" in his life. In the spotlight of the Council, though he was still only in his late 30s, he became one of the world's best-known young theologians. And his reputation in those years was as a "progressive," because in many matters he argued that Rome's curial bureaucracy had impeded the joyful and courageous proclamation of the Gospel to the world. "For the majority of the Council Fathers, the reform proposed by the liturgical movement did not constitute a priority; indeed, for many of them it wasn't even a matter to be treated," he recalls. "For example, Cardinal Montini, who later as Paul VI would become the real Pope of the Council, presenting his thematic summary at the beginning of the conciliar proceedings, had said clearly that he saw no essential task for the Council in the area of liturgy. The liturgy and its reform had become, after the First World War, a pressing question only in France and Germany, and more precisely in the perspective of the purest possible restoration of the ancient Roman liturgy; to this was added the necessity of an active participation of the people in the liturgical event. These two countries were then, along with Belgium and Holland ... managed to obtain approval that a schema on the sacred liturgy should be drawn up. That this text became the first to be examined by the Council did not depend in any way on an increased interest for the liturgy on the part of the majority of the Council Fathers, but on the fact that the liturgy seemed unlikely to spark polemics ... It would never have occurred to any Father to see in this text a 'revolution' which would signify 'the end of the Middle ages,' as some theologians have argued since. Moreover, the entire matter was seen as a continuation of the reform launched by Pius X and carried forward with prudence, but also determination, by Pius XII."

In 1970, after the new Missal of Paul VI had been promulgated, he wrote: "The fact that, after a period of experimentations that had often profoundly disfigured the liturgy, we were going back to having a binding liturgical text was to be greeted as something certainly positive. But I was shocked by the prohibition of the old Missal, since such a thing had never occurred in the entire previous history of the liturgy."

For Ratzinger, the abrupt change in the Church's liturgy had tragic consequences which are still causing grave harm to the Church.

"I am persuaded that the ecclesial crisis in which we find ourselves today depends in large part on the collapse of the liturgy, which is sometimes conceived of as something in which it does not matter whether God exists and speaks to us and listens to us," he writes. "But if in the liturgy the communion of faith, the universal unity of the Church and her history, the mystery of the living Christ, no longer appear, where is it that the Church still appears in her spiritual substance?" If there is not a new liturgical movement in the Church to restore the universality and sacredness of the liturgy, the Church risks "dissolution into parties of every type."

After the Council, his love for his native Bavaria drew him back from Munster to the south after only 3 years, when he accepted the newly created second chair of Dogma at the University of Tübingen. Here, in the late 1960s, Benedict witnessed the subordination of religion to Marxist political ideology, as the wave of student uprisings swept across Europe, and Marxism quickly became the dominant intellectual system also at his university in Tübingen, indoctrinating not only his students but many of the faculty as well. "There was an exploitation by ideologies that were tyrannical, brutal, and cruel. That experience made it clear to me that the abuse of faith had to be resisted precisely if one wanted to uphold the will of the Council."

Meanwhile, the post-conciliar discussions continued, with Ratzinger traveling often to Rome. Joseph decided to move even farther south and in 1969 accepted the chair for dogma in Regensburg. Here he was again reunited with his brother, who was by now the choir director of the world-famous Regensburg cathedral choir.

Right at the beginning of his Regensburg years, he was

appointed to the International Papal Theological Commission. This commission was intended to implement the new function that the Council had assigned to theologians and ensure that modern theological developments entered from the outset into the decision-making process of bishops and the Holy See.

In 1972, together with Hans Urs von Balthasar, Henri de Lubac, and others, he launched the Catholic theological journal *Communio*, a quarterly review of Catholic theology and culture. It has been said that this was done in response to the misinterpretation of the Second Vatican Council by Karl Rahner, Hans Kung, and others, who were represented by the theological journal *Concilium.*

After the death of the cardinal archbishop of Munich, Ratzinger was appointed to become archbishop by Pope Paul VI. He hesitantly wrote his acceptance letter. The day of his consecration was March 24, 1977. "That day was extraordinarily beautiful. It was a splendid summer day, the vigil of Pentecost. The cathedral in Munich ... was splendidly decorated and filled with a joyous atmosphere that was irresistible. I experienced what a sacrament is—that what occurs in a sacrament is reality ... the joy of the day was something really different from approval of a particular person, whose qualifications still have to be demonstrated. It was joy over the fact that this office, this service, was again present in a person who does not act and live for himself but for Him and therefore for all."

As his motto, he took a phrase from the *Third Letter of John,* Chapter 1, verse 8: "Let us be co-workers of the truth" (*"Cooperatores Veritatis"*).

Only 30 days later he was created cardinal by Pope Paul VI. In 1980, he was named by Pope John Paul II to chair the special Synod on the Laity. Shortly after that, the Pope asked him to head the Congregation for Catholic Education, which he declined, feeling he shouldn't leave his post in Munich too soon. But on November 25, 1981, he was named the Prefect for the Congregation for the Doctrine of the Faith.

> "I am still certain that the Lord prevails and that the Church survives, not only survives, but lives with strength through all of these crises. I am in this sense optimistic, because I am one who has the hope of the faith."
>
> —*Pope Benedict XVI,*
> *unpublished conversation with Robert Moynihan, March 23, 1993*

"How do you judge your own work?" I asked Pope Benedict some years ago, in a conversation in his office at the Congregation for the Doctrine of the Faith. "Some of your critics say you are too harsh in your defense of the faith. Others say you are not vigilant enough, that distortions of Church teaching are widespread and never corrected. What do you think? Too harsh . . . or too lenient?"

Cardinal Ratzinger thought for a moment. "This is really the question of many faithful," he replied. "Does the Church still teach anything, or not? It is a reason for us to examine our consciences, no?

"We are always being attacked for being inquisitors. People say we suppress freedom of thought, and so forth. But there is another criticism: that, on the contrary, we do not do our duty to protect the faithful. I would say that this is a matter others must judge.

"There are some criticisms: that we have sometimes been perhaps a little too over-scrupulous. Or that we have acted in ways that are against the Gospels, as Kung claims, as many claim. Or that we should simply not exist, that 'the wheat' and 'the weeds' should be allowed to grow up together.

"And this criticism is perhaps in continuity with my own thought, and of my trust in the Lord, who said to us: 'Let the wheat and the tares grow together. You are not in a position yourselves to cleanse this field.' Not in the sense of letting everything go, but in the sense that we cannot follow everything and purify everything.

"We have to do two things. We must do what we can to allow the light of the faith to shine forth, so that it may be evident that there *is* a doctrine, there *is* a faith, and that the faith is *this* . . . It seems to me that this is the first point.

"If there is not a positive exposition, in which one sees 'Look, this is the faith,' any attempt at surveillance over distortions of the faith will occur in a void.

"Therefore, this seems to me the first duty: to set forth our faith. And we have done something essential, in this regard, in publishing the *Catechism of the Catholic Church* (in the fall of 1992) so that one can really see: 'Yes, the Church has a doctrine, and her doctrine is this.'

"The second point is: we must support as much as we possibly can the entire network of responsibility in the Church. To me, it would be a mistaken conception of the primacy if Rome had to correct everything.

"No, Rome must commit herself, together with the college of bishops, to see to it that there are shepherds who all really, together, and in the great communion of the saints and in their responsibility before the Lord, act in the fear of the Lord, not out of fear of men. They must act together to make possible a faith that is free. And they must act in unison to bring clarity when there has been deception, when a human word is presented as a word of faith.

"What I mean is that we must not depend entirely on the primacy. We must strengthen all of the elements in the Church, all of those in positions of authority, so that they function smoothly."

Conservative or Radical?

"Are they right," I asked, "those who say that you are an 'ultra-conservative'?"

"I would say the work is conservative," Ratzinger replied, "in the sense that we must preserve the deposit of the faith, as Holy Scripture says. We must conserve it. But conserving the deposit of the faith is always to nourish an explosive force against the powers of this world that threaten justice, and threaten the poor."

"That sounds as if you are conservative and radical at once. But few would say that about you. Do you think you have been misunderstood?"

"By a certain part of the media, certainly, yes."

"Does this cause you to suffer?"

"Up to a certain point, yes," Ratzinger said. "But, on the other hand, I am a bit of a fatalist. The world is what it is. And it lives on the basis of simplified images . . ."

A deep contradiction has marked Benedict's life. He wished to be a scholar, a man of books and study, yet he was compelled to give up scholarship and become a Church official, an administrator. All of the Church advancements he has obtained—even this final one, to the throne of Peter—have been against his own will for his life.

The man who most influenced Benedict's thought, St.

Augustine, had a similar problem. "Augustine had chosen the life of a scholar," Benedict writes in his *Memoirs*, looking to Augustine's life to understand his own. "But God had destined him to become a 'beast of burden,' the sturdy ox who draws the cart of God in this world." Benedict saw that as his own fate as well: to be a type of "donkey" or "pack animal," carrying the burdens God had set upon his back.

The Greatness of St. Augustine

"Among your teachers, who has had the greatest influence on your intellectual and spiritual formation?" I asked him. "St. Augustine?"

"Always the great master, yes," he replied.

"He was the most influential on your formation?"

"Without a doubt, yes. He has had a very great influence on my thinking and I will always regard him as my great teacher.

"But, naturally, I then also began to study others: Bonaventure. Also Thomas Aquinas. Also the Greek Fathers, particularly Gregory of Nyssa."

The Study of God's Word

"Above all, I must say, I have always studied a great deal of exegesis—the interpretation of scripture. Because, precisely by Augustine himself, I was led to the scriptures. For this reason, for me, it was always fundamental and still is, to study and meditate profoundly on God's word.

"And this is the reason I have become so engaged in the battle over exegesis, over how to interpret scripture.

"I have learned from modern biblical exegesis, but I have also learned that it is not enough to enter into the fullness of the scripture. For this reason, I have always sought to combine a sound critical exegesis with the grand exegesis of the Fathers, that is, theological exegesis.

"This supposes the unity of the Scriptures and supposes also the 'ecclesiality' of the Scriptures, an ecclesial and liturgical reading of the Scriptures.

"This study of the Scriptures is still for me, together with reflection on the liturgy—the two coincide, for the liturgy *is* the great theme of the Scriptures, is a part of the Church—almost the fulcrum point of my theological work. My search is to find the way to determine the real contribution of critical exegesis and integrate it with the liturgical-ecclesial reading of Scripture."

The Struggle between the Faith and Modernity

"And it seems to me the whole struggle between modernity and true ecclesiality and also the struggle over the true intentions of the Second Vatican Council is concentrated here. Because here is the problem: Ought we to accept modernity in full, or in part? Is there a real contribution? Can this modern way of thinking be a contribution, or offer a contribution, or not? And if there is a contribution from the modern, critical way of thinking, in line with the Enlightenment, how can it be reconciled with the great intuitions and the great gifts of the faith?

"Or ought we, in the name of the faith, to reject modernity? You see? There always seems to be this dilemma: either we must reject the whole of the tradition, all the exegesis of the Fathers, relegate it to the library as historically unsustainable, or we must reject modernity.

"And I think that the gift, the light of the faith, must be dominant, but the light of the faith has also the capacity to take up into itself the true human lights, and for this reason the struggles over exegesis and the liturgy for me must be inserted into this great, let us call it epochal, struggle over how Christianity, over how the Christian responds to modernity, to the challenge of modernity."

"You use the phrase 'epochal struggle' . . ." I said.

"Yes."

"Well, at the very least, that means it is a struggle of enormous historical importance . . ."

"Yes, certainly . . ."

The "true" intent of Vatican II: to "heal modernity"

"And it seems to me," he continued, "that this was the true intention of the Second Vatican Council, to go beyond an unfruitful and overly narrow apologetic to a true synthesis with the positive elements of modernity, but at the same time, let us say, to transform modernity, to heal it of its illnesses, by means of the light and strength of the faith.

"Because it was the Council Fathers' intention to heal and transform modernity, and not simply to succumb to it or merge with it, the interpretations which interpret the Second Vatican Council in the sense of de-sacralization or profanation are erroneous.

"That is, Vatican II must not be interpreted as desiring a rejection of the tradition and an adapting of the Church to modernity and so causing the Church to become empty because it loses the word of faith."

The need to heal the secular world

"Augustine, as you know, was a man who, on the one hand, had studied in great depth the great philosophies, the profane literature of the ancient world.

"On the other hand, he was also *very* critical of the pagan authors, even with regard to Plato, to Virgil, those great authors whom he loved so much.

"He criticized them, and with a penetrating sense, purified them.

"This was his way of using the great pre-Christian culture: purify it, heal it, and in this way, also, healing it, he gave true greatness to this culture. Because in this way, it entered into the fact of the incarnation, no? And became part of the Word's incarnation.

"But only by means of the difficult process of purification, of transformation, of conversion.

"I would say the word 'conversion' is the key word, one of the key words, of St. Augustine, and our culture also has a need for conversion. Without conversion one does not arrive at the Lord. This is true of the individual, and this is true of the culture as well . . ."

And so to Rome . . .

John Paul II, who was elected Pope in 1978, told Ratzinger early on that he would invite him to Rome, to serve in the Roman curia. "The Pope told me he intended to summon me to Rome. I spelled out the reasons against it and he said: 'Let's think about it a bit longer.' Then, after the assassination attempt (May 13, 1981), we spoke about it again and he repeated that he felt he had to stick to his original decision. I objected that I felt so bound to theology that I desired to have the right to continue to publish works of a private nature and didn't know whether that would be compatible with this new task."

But it turned out that other Roman prefects had written

as private theologians in the past, so Ratzinger's desire to continue writing was no impediment.

Ratzinger did not become just any curial official. He took up the post of "Prefect of the Congregation for the Doctrine of the Faith," the highest doctrinal office in the Church next to that of the Pope himself. Ratzinger thus became the figure in the Roman Curia whose task it was to propose the Christian faith to a world which had, on the one hand, grown callous and indifferent (atheism, relativism, nihilism) and, on the other, become anti-rational and "enthusiastic" (for example, the "New Age" movements, which Ratzinger would call a "new Gnosticism").

In a series of intellectual and spiritual conflicts during the 1980s and 1990s, each with far-reaching social and political implications, Ratzinger implemented a carefully thought-out plan for the intellectual and spiritual renewal of Christianity.

In so doing, he exposed himself to ferocious attacks from critics who named him the *"Panzer Kardinal"* and charged that he was misinterpreting the Christian message and dividing the Church.

His fiercest critics described him as a distant, detached "inquisitor" caught up in the trappings of power.

His defenders responded that he was in no way the cruel inquisitor, but a quiet, gentle, "professor" with an air of serenity and holiness.

For Ratzinger, the modern world presents two faces or aspects. On the one hand, science has brought man undreamt of powers over nature, even over his own genetic code. But, at the same time, Ratzinger has argued, the stripping away of ancient pieties and the rejection of old attitudes of religious reverence for human life and the human person, taught by Christianity—and also by other traditional religions—has left modern man exposed to very grave dangers.

Ratzinger fears, for individual men and women, that they will be unable to find meaning and hope in this world where God is absent, and, for society in general, that by "clearing the decks" of anything divine, anything sacred, in our modern rejection of God, we may have prepared the world for the emergence of a more cruel and dangerous tyranny than any we have ever seen.

It is this danger that Ratzinger set his face against during his 25 years as Prefect of the Faith in Rome.

The motto on Ratzinger's coat of arms was taken from the Third Letter of the Apostle John: "Co-workers of the truth." It is a motto that sums up his life work: to speak the truth in love, in season and out of season, against opposition and incomprehension, with humility and courage.

Too negative?

Every court needs at least one person in it who will tell the truth. All courts, like all governments of any type, run this grave risk: that the members of the court, fearful of "rocking the boat," fearful of irritating the ruler, the chief executive, "the boss," will remain silent even in the face of real problems that have arisen and need to be addressed. In the court that is Vatican City, the voice that for 25 years was unafraid to face real problems and, consequently, the voice that has often been criticized as "too negative," "too pessimistic," was that of Cardinal Ratzinger.

In the early 1980s, it was Ratzinger who dared to raise his voice against the overwhelming liberal consensus that the

Second Vatican Council (1962–1965) had ushered in a "new springtime" in the Church. In his 1984 book-length interview with Vittorio Messori, *The Ratzinger Report*, the German cardinal expressed his concerns with what was, for the time, astonishing frankness: "It is time to find again the courage of nonconformism," he said, "the capacity to oppose many of the trends of the surrounding culture, renouncing a certain euphoric post-conciliar solidarity."

It was this non-conformist courage that Ratzinger virtually alone seemed to express. And it was in this context that, in that same 1984 interview, Ratzinger called for—to the dismay of many—a "restoration" of Catholic doctrine and discipline that would "close the first phase of the post-conciliar period."

Ratzinger was attacked by progressives who claimed the word "restoration," with all of its negative connotations— the restoration of monarchies in early modern European history, for example—should never have been uttered.

As time passed, Ratzinger slowly backed away from the term "restoration" and began to speak of the pressing need, not for a "restoration" but for a "reform of the reform." That phrase has, in the years since 1984, become his characteristic phrase. By it, he means pruning back the excesses and exaggerations in Catholic life and thought that have entered the Church since 1965, and "restoring" perennial, orthodox, faith and practice.

The friendship of John Paul II and Ratzinger

In an interview with German journalist Peter Seewald in 1996, Ratzinger described his relationship to Pope John Paul II.

"It is said," Seewald began, "that the Pope sometimes is afraid of you and that he has sometimes exclaimed: 'For goodness sake, what would Cardinal Ratzinger say'?"

Amused, Ratzinger replied that the Pope may have said that in a joking way, but that "he certainly isn't afraid of me!"

For 25 years, John Paul and Ratzinger met every Friday evening. Here is how Ratzinger described a typical meeting: "I wait, then the Pope comes in, we shake hands and we sit at the table. We exchange a few words of a personal nature having nothing to do with theology. Then I usually present the most pressing issues, the Pope asks questions, and we exchange ideas."

On certain issues, John Paul did not form a judgment until after he had heard from Ratzinger.

"For example, on the issue of how the Anglican converts were to be received," Ratzinger recalled. "To do this, the right juridical forms needed to be found. He didn't get too involved in the specifics, saying only: 'Be open.'"

On other issues, John Paul was intensely involved. "For example," Ratzinger said, "everything having to do with morality, with bioethics, social ethics, anything having to do with philosophy. All of these matters interest him very personally and so on these points some very intense dialogues arose." The discussions took place in German, which John Paul spoke well.

No measurable results

Ratzinger never imagined he would single-handedly change the direction of history. "The Lord's ways do not lead rapidly to measurable results," Ratzinger told Seewald. "When the disciples asked Jesus what was happening, he replied with the parable of the mustard seed, of the leaven, and many similar parables."

Ratzinger seems to accept the fact that coming decades and centuries may find the Church increasingly under cultural and political pressure, as in the first centuries. "Perhaps we must abandon the ideas of national or mass churches," Ratzinger says. "It is likely that there lies before us a different epoch in the history of the Church, a new epoch in which Christianity will find itself in the situation of the mustard seed, in tiny groups apparently without influence which nevertheless live intensely bearing witness against evil and bringing good into the world. I see a great movement of this type already underway."

What hope for renewal does he see? Not in the revival of an "ancient and sclerotic system" but in the recognition of the Church as "something fresh and desirable, something truly grand."

But only those who have succeeded in "transcending the experience of modernity" will be able to see this.

Ratzinger's vision is of a future when "modernity" no longer sets the intellectual or spiritual agenda, the framework for conceiving of alternatives ("faith" vs. "reason," "science" vs. "religion"), but is left behind entirely.

In this sense, Ratzinger's vision is a truly radical one: "modernity" and "post-modernity" are no longer concepts on his intellectual screen; "modernity" is already surpassed by the Christian worldview that is emerging out of the depths of the post-conciliar crisis. "We must become ever more aware of the fact that we no longer know what Christianity is," Ratzinger said. "To give an example: how many images within a church no longer mean anything to most people? No one knows any more what they signify. Even concepts which were still familiar a generation ago, like 'tabernacle,' have become foreign."

What is needed in this situation? "A new curiosity about Christianity, a desire to understand what it really is." And what is Christianity, really? Not a theology, a collection of ideas, but an event, a fact: the Incarnation and the death of Christ on the cross.

"The essential is not that Christ announced certain ideas—something that he in fact did, of course—but that I become a Christian in the measure to which I believe in this event: God entered the world and acted," Ratzinger told Seewald.

Ratzinger's personal "models" are individuals who "listen to their consciences" and place what is good and right above "the approval of the many"—men like Thomas More, John Henry Newman, and the Protestant pastor persecuted by the Nazis, Dietrich Bonhoeffer.

"My deepest purpose," Ratzinger told Seewald, "especially during the Council, was always to free the true core of the faith from encrustations, to restore to it energy and dynamism. This impulse is the true constant in my life. For me, the important thing is not ever to have deviated from this constant that characterizes my life from my infancy, and to have remained faithful to the fundamental direction of my life."

Single combats

Cardinal Joseph Ratzinger arrived in Rome in January 1982. For the next 25 years he was Pope John Paul II's chief doctrinal officer, and now he has succeeded John Paul as Pope Benedict XVI. It seems certain now that he will live out his life in Rome. Ratzinger's Roman years have been marked by a series of profoundly important theological conflicts. Each of the conflicts seemed to pit Ratzinger against a single theologian, so that the 1980s and 1990s seemed to be a series of single combats before doctrinal truth between a series of bold theologians and the prefect of the faith in Rome. These conflicts were closely followed in the press and sometimes literally erupted into spectacular media events. The result was that Ratzinger became the most well known name in the Catholic Church after that of Wojtyla himself.

The "Absence" of God

The "golden thread" that explains why Ratzinger chose to fight the battles he did is the conviction that the great crisis of our time is the "absence of God."

For Ratzinger, all of modern history is marked by this progressive "departure" of God, of the transcendent, of the Sacred, from personal and social life. In a word, the world has become "secularized."

The word "secularized" means "conformed to the *saeculum*" that is, to be completely divided from everything having to do with God, the Sacred, and the Holy.

The *"saeculum"* is the word the Romans used to describe the entire material universe. It meant literally "this age."

In Christian belief, there is "another age" which is to come and which is known as the "Kingdom of God." These concepts are worked out in great profundity in the theology of St. Augustine, and Ratzinger was, as we have seen, deeply influenced by St. Augustine. The analysis of modernity as a period of relentless "secularization" is the principle key to understanding Ratzinger's mind. Ratzinger has bent all his intellect and will toward discovering a way to stop and to reverse this "secularizing" process. And this has set him squarely against the vast majority of the great intellects of our age.

The process of "secularization" is, of course, an immensely complex one and it would be wrong to oversimplify it, but it is not entirely false to say that the great prophets of secularism were the philosophers of the French enlightenment, the liberal humanist philosophers of England, and the three pivotal founders of intellectual schools: Karl Marx (communism), Charles Darwin (evolution on the basis of natural selection), and Sigmund Freud (psychoanalysis of the unconscious mind).

In the intellectual world created by the thought of Marx, Darwin, and Freud, elements of whose ideas have become all pervasive, even for ordinary people, at the beginning of the 21st century due to the popularization of their ideas, there is little room for any concept of "God."

Political life, for true communists, is reduced to the ideological clashes of economic classes moved purely by economic interest. The development of all life, and of human life in particular, for Darwinists, is a deterministic process, ruled by chance and dependent on almost infinite space and time. And, for Freudians, the human mind and consciousness is said to be understood entirely as the product of hormonal drives and infantile repressions and obsessions. For Benedict, these philosophers of secularism have "sown the wind, and reaped the whirlwind."

The ideologies of the 20th century, with their fierce conviction of historical purpose—they "knew" that they were "right" and that history was "on their side"—most notably National Socialism, Fascism, and Communism, carried out some of the greatest atrocities against human persons the world has ever seen.

Benedict, having lived through this terror and having experienced in his own life the arrogance of the Nazis and listened nightly to his father's criticism of their barbaric behavior, is persuaded that humanity must change course or face even greater atrocities and barbarism in the decades to come. It is this conviction of the looming threat of new anti-human ideologies and philosophies which has caused him to undertake the battles he has fought so relentlessly.

His work has centered on three key major battles: in the 1980s, the battle over liberation theology, where his watchword was Christian "freedom" over against Marxist "liberation"; in the 1990s and into the new millennium, the battle over relativism, where his watchword was "truth exists" over against "there is no truth"; finally, from 1982 through 2005, a series of battles over the Church's way of worshipping God, which in the Catholic Church is called "the liturgy"—that whole complex of prayers, actions, and rituals which comprise the Church's adoration of God, those actions which show the Church's love of God, and of their fellow believers—where his watchwords have been "communion" and "love" over against false understandings of Christian worship and communion with God and others.

Thus, in the years from 1981 to 2005, Ratzinger's work was a calculated defense of the Christian view of man, society, and the universe—of freedom, truth, and love—over against the dominant secular outlook of our time.

Liberation theology

"Liberation theology" is the term used to describe a theological school with roots in Europe and branches in Latin America, Africa, Asia—everywhere in the world. An essential idea of liberation theology is that Christian faith must not be restricted to studying the Bible and worshipping God in Church services, but must engage in a political and social struggle to bring about a better, more just human society. The essential danger of liberation theology, in Ratzinger's view, is that precisely this emphasis on "results" in this world can tempt the liberation theologians to take a Machiavellian turn, and justify violence, even against innocent people, in order for "the cause" to succeed.

In short, the person is swallowed up, and sometimes trampled under, by an "ideology" with a single-minded goal. Liberation theologians also use Marxist categories to describe the relations inside the Church as a type of "class struggle" between the laity and the clergy. This "politicization" of the mystical life of the Church was of particular concern to Ratzinger. He felt it was a wrong understanding of Christian life and Christian vocations to the priesthood, and that it introduced "worldly" criteria of judgment into an analysis of inner Church (ecclesial) relations. For this reason, he said liberation theology often has a false "ecclesiology," a false understanding of what the Church is, how she is organized, and where she is going and why.

The battle over liberation theology came to a head in 1984. In that year, a young Franciscan theologian from Brazil named Leonardo Boff, who had written eloquently about the need for social justice in Brazilian society, and within the Catholic Church, was invited to Rome by Ratzinger for a "conversation."

The world's press went wild. Boff, in his Franciscan robe and wearing a full beard, seemed at once a dashing and a prophetic figure. The media loved him. Ratzinger, with his quiet, reserved, Germanic demeanor, seemed cast by Hollywood to play the role of the "Grand Inquisitor" who would "interrogate" and perhaps punish the bold, creative, vibrant Brazilian theologian.

Boff had written a book in 1981, at the age of 41, called *Church: Charism and Power: Liberation Theology and the Institutional Church*. In it, Boff had written: "Sacred power has been the object of a process of expropriation of the means of religious production on the part of the clergy, to the detriment of the Christian people." He had gone on to attack the "pyramidal power of the Vatican." The diocesan commission of the Church in Rio de Janeiro had criticized the book. Boff wrote a reply to the criticisms, and on February 12, 1982, sent the reply also to Rome. Ratzinger had just taken his post, so this case was the very first new case he encountered on the job. He read Boff's writings, and the criticisms of them, and Boff's response to the criticism. On May 15, Ratzinger wrote to Boff, saying a few of the criticisms seemed valid to him. Ratzinger said Boff's critique of the Church structure was marked by "radical aggression." He asked: "Is your reasoning in these pages guided by the faith, or by principles of an ideological nature inspired in part by Marxism?" Ratzinger ended by inviting Boff to have a "conversation" to "clarify" things. Boff agreed. The date was fixed for September 7, 1984.

"Would you like a cup of coffee?"

At 9:40 A.M. that day, a black Volkswagen with a Vatican license plate arrived at the Franciscan General Curia in Rome to pick up Boff and bring him to the meeting with Ratzinger. Boff, joking, held out his hands and said: "You could handcuff me." The car returned to the Vatican. With

Ratzinger was Monsignor Jorge Mejia, today a cardinal. The conversation got underway. The climate was relaxed and friendly.

At a certain point, Ratzinger looked at Boff and asked: "Would you like a cup of coffee? You must be tired..." Boff agreed.

Their conversation was halted as the men drank coffee. As they did so, Ratzinger remarked on Boff's long Franciscan robe: "You look well in that robe, father. Also in this way you can give a sign to the world."

"It is quite difficult to wear this robe," Boff replied, "because it is so hot in our part of the world."

"But for this reason, the people will see your devotion and patience and say: he is paying for the sins of the world," Ratzinger said.

"Certainly we need signs of transcendence," Boff replied. "But they are not given by a robe. It is the heart that must be set right."

"Hearts cannot be seen," Ratzinger replied. "Something must be made a visible sign."

"This habit can also be a sign of power," Boff said. "When I am wearing it and get onto a city bus, the people get up and say, 'Have my seat, padre.' But we must be servants."

The coffee break ended and the discussion continued. It lasted for three hours. And the next day, the world's press was filled with accounts of Boff's "inquisition"—and of the coffee break where the cardinal asked the friar to wear his order's robe.

On March 21, 1985, the Vatican newspaper, *Osservatore Romano*, published a "notification" on Boff's book. "We feel obliged to declare that the options of Leonardo Boff here analyzed are of such a nature as to place in danger the doctrine of the faith, which this Congregation has the task of promoting and defending." Certain points in Boff's writings were judged "untenable." On April 26, Boff was asked to keep a year of silence before writing further on the matter. Boff agreed. In 1992, he lost his teaching post and shortly thereafter left the Franciscan order.

Document on Liberation Theology

On August 6, 1984, Ratzinger issued his *Instruction on Certain Aspects of the "Theology of Liberation."* His main point: to warn against a "false liberation" from evident social evils which would prevent people from embracing the "true liberation" offered by Jesus Christ.

"Liberation," he wrote, "is first and foremost liberation from the radical slavery of sin. Its end and its goal is the freedom of the children of God, which is the gift of grace. As a logical consequence, it calls for freedom from many different kinds of slavery in the cultural, economic, social, and political spheres, all of which derive ultimately from sin, and so often prevent people from living in a manner befitting their dignity."

He then added, referring to Marxist analysis: "Faced with the urgency of certain problems, some are tempted to emphasize, unilaterally, the liberation from servitude of an earthly and temporal kind. They do so in such a way that they seem to put liberation from sin in second place, and so fail to give it the primary importance it is due. Thus, their very presentation of the problems is confused and ambiguous. Others, in an effort to learn more precisely what are the causes of the slavery which they want to end, make use of different concepts without sufficient critical caution."

He summed up his attitude toward the issue with these

words: "This warning should in no way be interpreted as a disavowal of all those who want to respond generously and with an authentic evangelical spirit to the 'preferential option for the poor.' It should not at all serve as an excuse for those who maintain the attitude of neutrality and indifference in the face of the tragic and pressing problems of human misery and injustice. It is, on the contrary, dictated by the certitude that the serious ideological deviations which it points out tends inevitably to betray the cause of the poor."

He then issued this challenge: "More than ever, it is important that numerous Christians, whose faith is clear and who are committed to live the Christian life in its fullness, become involved in the struggle for justice, freedom, and human dignity because of their love for their disinherited, oppressed, and persecuted brothers and sisters. More than ever, the Church intends to condemn abuses, injustices, and attacks against freedom, wherever they occur and whoever commits them. She intends to struggle, by her own means, for the defense and advancement of the rights of mankind, especially of the poor."

The problem, in Ratzinger's view, was that Boff and other liberation theologians had mistaken the real core of the problem, which, he said, lies in the will of the individual person, and not in oppressive social structures: "Nor can one localize evil principally or uniquely in bad social, political, or economic 'structures' as though all other evils came from them so that the creation of the 'new man' would depend on the establishment of different economic and sociopolitical structures. To be sure, there are structures which are evil and which cause evil and which we must have the courage to change. Structures, whether they are good or bad, are the result of man's actions and so are consequences more than causes. The root of evil, then, lies in free and responsible persons who have to be converted by the grace of Jesus Christ in order to live and act as new creatures in the love of neighbor and in the effective search for justice, self-control, and the exercise of virtue."

In mistaking the origin of the problem, they had also mistaken the true solution: the presence of God. For Ratzinger, "the feeling of anguish at the urgency of the problems cannot make us lose sight of what is essential nor forget the reply of Jesus to the Tempter: 'It is not on bread alone that man lives, but on every word that comes from the mouth of God' (Matthew 4:4; cf. Deuteronomy 8:3). Faced with the urgency of sharing bread, some are tempted to put evangelization into parentheses, as it were, and postpone it until tomorrow: first the bread, then the Word of the Lord. It is a fatal error to separate these two and even worse to oppose the one to the other. In fact, the Christian perspective naturally shows they have a great deal to do with one another. To some it even seems that the necessary struggle for human justice and freedom in the economic and political sense constitutes the whole essence of salvation. For them, the Gospel is reduced to a purely earthly gospel."

The liberation theologians had also gone astray in using categories of Marxist analysis which, for Ratzinger, were intrinsically misleading because rooted in atheism—in that very "absence of God" which he believed was the true source of the problem. He wrote: "Let us recall the fact that atheism and the denial of the human person, his liberty and rights, are at the core of the Marxist theory. This theory, then, contains errors which directly threaten the truths of the faith regarding the eternal destiny of individual persons. Moreover, to attempt to integrate into theology an analysis whose criterion of interpretation depends on this atheistic conception is to involve oneself in terrible contradictions. What is more, this misunderstanding of the spiritual nature of the person leads to a total subordination of the person to the collectivity, and thus to the denial of the principles of a social and political life which is in keeping with human dignity."

Indeed, Ratzinger argues, this type of theology eventually transforms the basic Christian teachings on faith, hope, and love into something completely alien to the Christian tradition: "Along these lines, some go so far as to identify God Himself with history and to define faith as 'fidelity to history,' which means adhering to a political policy which is suited to the growth of humanity, conceived as a purely temporal messianism. As a consequence, faith, hope, and charity are given a new content: they become 'fidelity to history,' 'confidence in the future,' and 'option for the poor.' This is tantamount to saying they have been emptied of their theological reality."

The end result, for Ratzinger, is that Christian love, and Christian communion in the Eucharist, is shattered. This theology, in short, dismantles the very thing Christianity seeks to do: bring about a community of love. He writes: "As a result, participation in the class struggle is presented as a requirement of charity itself. The desire to love everyone here and now, despite his class, and to go out to meet him with the nonviolent means of dialogue and persuasion, is denounced as counterproductive and opposed to love. If one holds that a person should not be the object of hate, it is claimed nevertheless that, if he belongs to the objective class of the rich, he is primarily a class enemy to be fought. Thus the universality of love of neighbor and brotherhood become an eschatological principle, which will only have meaning for the 'new man,' who arises out of the victorious revolution. As far as the Church is concerned, this system would see her 'only' as a reality interior to history, herself subject to those laws which are supposed to govern the development of history in its immanence. The Church, the gift of God and mystery of faith, is emptied of any specific reality by this reductionism. At the same time, it is disputed that the participation of Christians who belong to opposing classes at the same Eucharistic Table still makes any sense."

Ratzinger was at pains to make clear that his criticisms of Boff's theology did not mean he was tolerant of political or economic oppression: "The warning against the serious deviations of some 'theologies of liberation' must not be taken as some kind of approval, even indirect, of those who keep the poor in misery, who profit from that misery, who notice it while doing nothing about it, or who remain indifferent to it. The Church, guided by the Gospel of mercy and by the love for mankind, hears the cry for justice and intends to respond to it with all her might."

And yet, he was adamant that the struggle against injustice had to be waged, insofar as possible, nonviolently: "The truth of mankind requires that this battle be fought in ways consistent with human dignity. That is why the systematic and deliberate recourse to blind violence, no matter from which side it comes, must be condemned. To put one's trust in violent means in the hope of restoring more justice is to become the victim of a fatal illusion: violence begets violence and degrades man. It mocks the dignity of man in the person of the victims and it debases that same dignity among those who practice it."

A Chance Encounter

By chance, I was in Rome in September of 1984, and happened to run into Cardinal Ratzinger one morning in St. Peter's Square. I knew he had just seen Boff, because of the massive press coverage.

I had another matter to discuss with him, nothing to do with Boff. It had to do with my own research in the Vatican library into the early history of the Franciscan order, and into the influence of the thought of the Calabrian Abbot Joachim of Fiore (1135–1202) on the early Franciscans. Joachim had taught that a "new age" of "the Holy Spirit" was about to arrive in the 1200s, an age of justice, and some of the early Franciscans were radicalized by this vision, expecting a complete change in the structures of society and the Church.

Ratzinger's *habilitationschrift*—the one he had such trouble getting approved—had dealt precisely with these questions, specifically, with the way St. Bonaventure, himself a Franciscan, had integrated Joachim's thought into his own theology of history.

So, as we walked across St. Peter's Square, we discussed Joachim and Bonaventure. And when we parted, I ventured that "the arguments of the liberation theologians today seem to echo some of the arguments of the Joachites in the 1200s . . ."

And the cardinal replied, "Yes, precisely. The spiritual Franciscans of that time and the liberation theologians of today share much in common."

Relativism

The battle against relativism was the second key theme of Ratzinger's work from 1982 to 2005. This battle often involved issues in sexual morality, but it also involved ecumenism and the question of whether a religious belief can be "true" for all men, and not "relative."

Already on March 27, 1982, Ratzinger was criticizing the work of the commission dealing with dialogue between Anglicans and Catholics for "lack of clarity" on a number of theological points. In his remarks, he said "we agreed to disagree."

In 1983, Ratzinger opened an investigation of Archbishop Raymond Hunthausen, of Seattle, Washington, for his views on women, homosexuality, and a number of other doctrinal issues. Ratzinger decided on an unusual remedy for Hunthausen's dissent: he sent an assistant bishop to run some aspects of the diocese. Hunthausen came to Rome and had a 13-hour meeting with Ratzinger. Ratzinger warned Hunthausen against politicizing the issue of women in the Church, using married ex-priests, marrying divorced people, and allowing them to receive communion, giving Holy Communion in ecumenical settings, and granting general absolution of sins to large groups.

Ratzinger did not restore Hunthausen's authority and issued a special warning on the problem of homosexuality: "The archdiocese should withdraw all support from any group which does not unequivocally accept the teaching of the magisterium concerning the intrinsic evil of homosexual activity . . . A compassionate ministry to homosexual persons must be developed that has as its clear goal the promotion of a chaste lifestyle. Particular care is to be exercised by any who represent the archdiocese, to explain clearly the position of the Church on this question."

In 1986 came the dispute with the American moral theologian from Catholic University of America in Washington,

D.C., Father Charles E. Curran, over issues of sexual morality (contraception, divorce, homosexuality). Curran, like Boff, came to Rome for a meeting with Ratzinger. He did not change his views, and later was removed from his teaching post at Catholic University.

From 1986–1992, Ratzinger was deeply involved in preparing the new (plain text) *Catechism of the Catholic Church.* Some observers regard the *Catechism* as the greatest single production of John Paul II's pontificate, and it was Ratzinger who shepherded this project to its conclusion. When it was published in America in 1994, after a long battle over inclusive language in the English translation which ended with inclusive language not being used, the *Catechism* was a best seller, selling many millions of copies.

On February 22, 1987, came a letter on bioethics entitled *Donum Vitae* (The Gift of Life) which dealt again with sexual and reproductive morality. The issue is of increasing importance, given the advances in the biomedical sciences, and is likely to be an issue during Benedict's pontificate.

The issue is of particular importance for those couples unable to conceive children. Ratzinger recognizes the terrible suffering this can cause a couple. "The suffering of spouses who cannot have children or who are afraid of bringing a handicapped child into the world is a suffering that everyone must understand," Ratzinger writes. "The desire for a child is natural: it expresses the vocation to fatherhood and motherhood inscribed in conjugal love. This desire can be even stronger if the couple is affected by sterility which appears incurable.

"Nevertheless," he continues, "marriage does not confer upon the spouses the right to have a child, but only the right to perform those natural acts which are per se ordered to procreation. A true and proper right to a child would be contrary to the child's dignity and nature. The child is not an object to which one has a right, nor can he be considered as an object of ownership: rather, a child is a gift, 'the supreme gift' and the most gratuitous gift of marriage, and is a living testimony of the mutual giving of his parents.

"For this reason, the child has the right, as already mentioned, to be the fruit of the specific act of the conjugal love of his parents; and he also has the right to be respected as a person from the moment of his conception."

Ratzinger in this document looks closely at all the issues involved in human procreation. "The fundamental values connected with the techniques of artificial human procreation are two: the life of the human being called into existence and the special nature of the transmission of human life in marriage," Ratzinger writes. "The moral judgment on such methods of artificial procreation must therefore be formulated in reference to these values ... Advances in technology have now made it possible to procreate apart from sexual relations through the meeting *in vitro* of the germ cells previously taken from the man and the woman. But what is technically possible is not for that very reason morally admissible."

The cardinal went on to argue that the human embryo, though incredibly small, weak, and undeveloped, has intrinsic dignity because it is human, and so must not be treated as simple tissue and subjected to experiments, or killed. He wrote: "The human being must be respected—as a person—from the very first instant of his existence. The implementation of procedures of artificial fertilization has made possible various interventions upon embryos and human fetuses. The aims pursued are of various kinds: diag-

nostic and therapeutic, scientific, and commercial. From all
of this, serious problems arise. Can one speak of a right to
experimentation upon human embryos for the purpose of
scientific research? What norms or laws should be worked
out with regard to this matter?"

In the end, the document takes a negative view of the
morality of *in vitro* fertilization. One of the reasons that
Ratzinger takes a negative view of this fertility technology
is because, he notes, it usually involves the conception of
several embryos, and the destruction of several. "In the cir-
cumstances in which it is regularly practiced, *in vitro* fertilization and embryo transfer involves the destruction of
human beings, which is something contrary to the doctrine
on the illicitness of abortion previously mentioned.

"But," he continues, "even in a situation in which every
precaution were taken to avoid the death of human embryos, homologous *in vitro* fertilization and embryo transfer
dissociates from the conjugal act the actions which are directed to human fertilization . . ."

What he is particularly concerned about, he says, is that
two human beings, a man and a woman, a married couple
who wish to have children, place their procreation in the
hands of technological experts. Ratzinger has often made
this point: that the "experts" are increasingly entering into
spheres where ordinary human beings ought to be free. He
evidently fears that the role of "experts" in the sexual lives
and procreational lives of human beings will increase dra-
matically in years to come, and that this could involve a loss
of privacy, autonomy, and freedom.

He writes: "*In vitro* fertilization and embryo transfer is
brought about outside the bodies of the couple through actions of third parties whose competence and technical

activity determine the success of the procedure. Such fertilization entrusts the life and identity of the embryo into the power of doctors and biologists and establishes the domination of technology over the origin and destiny of the human person. Such a relationship of domination is in itself contrary to the dignity and equality that must be common to parents and children."

In the end, *in vitro* fertilization, even within a marital relationship, is regarded as morally wrong. He writes: "Certainly, homologous *in vitro* fertilization and embryo transfer fertilization is not marked by all that ethical negativity found in extra-conjugal procreation; the family and marriage continue to constitute the setting for the birth and upbringing of the children. Nevertheless, in conformity with the traditional doctrine relating to the goods of marriage and the dignity of the person, the Church remains opposed from the moral point of view to homologous *in vitro* fertilization. Such fertilization is in itself illicit and in opposition to the dignity of procreation and of the conjugal union, even when everything is done to avoid the death of the human embryo."

But, he concludes: "Although the manner in which human conception is achieved with *in vitro* fertilization and embryo transfer cannot be approved, every child which comes into the world must in any case be accepted as a living gift of the divine Goodness and must be brought up with love."

In 1989, he published an "oath of fidelity" which he asked all Catholic bishops to take. He also published a document on oriental meditation and Buddhism, saying there was a risk of "relativizing" Christian truth in using eastern meditation techniques, like yoga. He also criticized some of the moral teachings of Father Bernhard Haring. Also in

1989, 163 theologians in Germany signed a document called the "Declaration of Cologne," saying that Rome, and Ratzinger especially, was impinging on the "academic freedom" of theologians.

Ratzinger responded in 1990 with *Donum veritatis ("The Gift of Truth"): On the Ecclesial Vocation of the Theologian*. He argued that Christian truth did not put academics in a straitjacket, but gave them a priceless compass for their research and reflection.

Throughout the 1990s, Ratzinger engaged in a running battle with German theologians over moral issues ranging from allowing divorced and remarried Catholics to receive communion, to keeping the Church from appearing to participate in or condone a German government bureaucratic ruling which allowed legalized abortion after consultation between the woman and a Church representative.

In order to reach out to a German audience, in the late 1990s he took the unusual step of conducting a book-length interview with the German journalist Peter Seewald, who published the interview under the title *Salz der Erde (Salt of the Earth)*. One of the key themes of the interview was the danger of relativism.

His work to refute relativism reached its high point with the publication of the controversial document, *Dominus Jesus* ("The Lord Jesus") on August 6 in the year 2000. Here is the key passage: "The Church's constant missionary proclamation is endangered today by relativistic theories which seek to justify religious pluralism, not only *de facto* but also *de iure* (or in principle). As a consequence, it is held that certain truths have been superseded; for example, the definitive and complete character of the revelation of Jesus Christ, the nature of Christian faith as compared with that of belief in

other religions ... The roots of these problems are to be
found in certain presuppositions of both a philosophical
and theological nature, which hinder the understanding and
acceptance of the revealed truth. Some of these can be mentioned: the conviction of the elusiveness and inexpressibility
of divine truth, even by Christian revelation; relativistic attitudes toward truth itself, according to which what is true for
some would not be true for others ..."

What especially disturbed many readers of this document was Ratzinger's decision to stress the centrality and
uniqueness of Jesus Christ. Ratzinger's decision seemed to
many in ecumenical circles to be "anti-ecumenical." But he
did not mince words: "In contemporary theological reflection there often emerges an approach to Jesus of Nazareth
that considers him a particular, finite, historical figure, who
reveals the divine not in an exclusive way, but in a way com-
plementary with other revelatory and salvific figures. The
Infinite, the Absolute, the Ultimate Mystery of God would
thus manifest itself to humanity in many ways and in many
historical figures: Jesus of Nazareth would be one of these.
More concretely, for some, Jesus would be one of the many
faces which the Logos has assumed in the course of time to
communicate with humanity in a salvific way."

Ratzinger made it clear that Christians could not be
"relativistic" about Jesus Christ and remain Christians.
"These theses are in profound conflict with the Christian
faith. The doctrine of faith must be *firmly believed* which pro-
claims that Jesus of Nazareth, son of Mary, and he alone,
is the Son and the Word of the Father." The Word, which
"was in the beginning with God" (/Jn/ 1:2) is the same as
he who "became flesh" (/Jn/ 1:14). In Jesus, "the Christ,
the Son of the living God" (/Mt/ 16:16), "the whole full-

ness of divinity dwells in bodily form" (/Col/ 2:9). He is the "only begotten Son of the Father, who is in the bosom of the Father" (/Jn/ 1:18), his "beloved Son, in whom we have redemption ... In him the fullness of God was pleased to dwell, and through him, God was pleased to reconcile all things to himself, on earth and in the heavens, making peace by the blood of his Cross" (/Col/ 1:13-14, 19-20).

But what caused the most outrage was that Ratzinger took the argument one step further and said that, not only was Jesus Christ unique, but so also was his "mystical body," the Church. And, he said, that Church was the Roman Catholic Church. This prompted many to say Ratzinger had stepped over the line into polemics.

Here is Ratzinger's argument: "The Lord Jesus, the only Savior, did not only establish a simple community of disciples, but constituted the Church as a salvific mystery: he himself is in the Church and the Church is in him (cf. Jn 15:1ff.; Gal 3:28; Eph 4:15-16; Acts 9:5). Therefore, the fullness of Christ's salvific mystery belongs also to the Church, inseparably united to her Lord. Indeed, Jesus Christ continues his presence and his work of salvation in the Church and by means of the Church (cf. Col 1:24-27), which is his body (cf. 1 Cor 12:12-13, 27; Col 1:18) ...

"Therefore, in connection with the unicity and universality of the salvific mediation of Jesus Christ, the unicity of the Church founded by him must be firmly believed as a truth of Catholic faith. Just as there is one Christ, so there exists a single body of Christ, a single Bride of Christ: 'a single Catholic and apostolic Church' ...

"The Catholic faithful are required to profess that there is an historical continuity—rooted in the apostolic succession—between the Church founded by Christ and the Catholic ...

This Church, constituted and organized as a society in the present world, subsists in [*subsistit in*] the Catholic Church, governed by the Successor of Peter and by the Bishops in communion with him."

In this regard, Ratzinger made one further remark, which particularly outraged some Protestants: "The ecclesial communities which have not preserved the valid Episcopate and the genuine and integral substance of the Eucharistic mystery are not Churches in the proper sense."

The worship of God

Worship. The word falls oddly on many modern ears. What does it mean "to worship"? To "adore"? Is it something one chooses to do as often as possible? Is it something one is forced to do on Sundays? Does it require a certain ritual, a certain behavior? Who is the one worshiped, and why? For Ratzinger, the worship of God is the most important, beautiful, fitting, joy-filled and satisfying—"life-giving" thing a human being can do. It is so, he believes, because God is "the" perfect being: eternal, holy, good, the source of all other beings and all life. As such, he is "worthy" of our "adoration"—and no other reality or being is. Only God is a fit "object" of human worship. It is this that the First of the Ten Commandments is revealing: no other "gods" are worthy of human worship. But the true God is.

To worship the true God is, for Ratzinger, to draw close to the ultimate source and meaning of everything in the universe, to be "in communion" with that source in prayer and in song and in other ritual acts, and therefore, in some way, to participate in the very life of that divine being who is worshiped. To "worship" God is, for Ratzinger, very near to the same thing—though it is not exactly the same thing—

as to "love" God. "To worship" and "to love" are intimately related, and intertwined.

Since this is so, Ratzinger believes that knowing how to pray, to worship, to enter into communion with God, to love God, and then, receiving back from God some portion, some particle, some semblance, of his divine life, becomes the single most important and wonderful thing a person can do in this world.

Many people in the pre-modern age believed this. This explains why so much time and effort and treasure was spent in centuries past on building great cathedrals, on adorning them with beautiful mosaics and paints, in building great mosques, and the Temple in Jerusalem, and religious institutions and structures of all types: because people believed that they could please God in this way, and draw close to him, and receive some grace from him, some gift, some life—even eternal life.

But, in the modern, secularized world, in the world where our great crisis is, as Ratzinger has argued, "the absence of God," religious worship is often a marginal matter, often left to old women and small children. The churches of the western world are closing. Some are becoming beer halls and discotheques. Many priests have left their priesthood, and few enter to replace them. And many people find it difficult to get up on Sunday morning and go to church, having lost the sense that in their Sunday worship, they draw close to God, and receiving back from him the "grace" leading to eternal life.

For almost 25 years, perhaps the chief concern of Ratzinger's work has been to "reform the reform" of Catholic worship, enabling the Church's worship to become the vibrant, intense, fruitful adoration of God that it was intended to be from the beginning.

The one schism

There has been only one open schism in the Roman Catholic Church since the Second Vatican Council (1962–65). It occurred in 1988. And it was perhaps Ratzinger's greatest single failure. The roots of the schism lay in the reform of the liturgy of the Catholic Church introduced after the Council, though there were other reasons besides liturgical ones for the schism. Of the nearly 3,000 bishops who attended the Council, only one, a Frenchman named Marcel Lefebvre, has publicly broken with Rome, taking with him some 200 priests and several hundred thousand Catholics from around the world. Lefebvre died in 1991, but his movement lives on, because Lefebvre ordained four bishops to succeed him in a ceremony on June 30, 1988—against the Pope's express will. It was this act of consecration, and of disobedience, which led to Lefebvre's excommunication, with the four bishops he consecrated, and so to the schism.

Already in the late 1960s, and throughout the 1970s, Lefebvre argued that Rome had made a mistake in eliminating the Latin language in the liturgy, and in changing the old prayers. And he gathered like-minded young men around him at a seminary in Econe, Switzerland. There, the old Latin liturgy, and other aspects of Church tradition, were not forgotten.

But the Lefebvrists had a problem. In 1976, Pope Paul VI had asked Lefebvre to stop ordaining priests he had trained in his seminary, and when Lefebvre resisted, Paul suspended him from acting as a priest. After Paul VI died, in 1978,

John Paul II became Pope. He hoped to solve the Lefebvre issue, but could not. Finally, in 1988, the Lefebvrists turned to Cardinal Ratzinger to find an understanding ear. Throughout the winter and spring of 1988, Ratzinger and Lefebvre, assisted by a small team of theological advisors, hammered out a "Protocol of Agreement" which provided a theological and juridical framework for the re-entry of Lefebvre and his followers into full communion with the Church.

That Protocol was signed on May 5, 1988 by both Ratzinger and Lefebvre. Under its terms, Lefebvre would have received back his priestly faculties and been granted the right to ordain a successor bishop. A 7-member Roman Commission would have been set up to oversee the community, with two of the seven members from the Lefebvrist community. In return, Lefebvre, somewhat grudgingly and provisionally, would have agreed to submit to Rome and to Rome's interpretation of the Second Vatican Council. ("We promise to be always faithful to the Catholic Church and to the Roman Pontiff, her Supreme Pastor," Lefebvre agreed. "With regard to certain points taught by the Second Vatican Council or concerning the later reforms of the liturgy and canon law, and which seem to us able to be reconciled with the Tradition only with difficulty, we commit ourselves to have a positive attitude of study and of communication with the Holy See, avoiding all polemics.")

For Ratzinger, the agreement was a personal triumph. Many in the Roman curia had not thought it would be possible (or had hoped it would not be) for Lefebvre to be reconciled with Rome. Ratzinger had succeeded in accomplishing the (nearly) impossible.

But only for one day. On the morning of May 6, 1988, Lefebvre sent a hand-written note to Ratzinger. The French archbishop insisted that the episcopal ordinations of his successors in the Society of St. Pius X should take place, as the Society had originally planned, on June 30, and that he should be allowed to ordain more than one bishop, since one would be insufficient to carry out all the work of the community, now present in many parts of the world. He also insisted that the Society be given a majority on the Roman Commission which would be set up to oversee it.

Rome had other thoughts. Vatican officials wanted Lefebvre to submit the names of his proposed candidates for the episcopacy to the Vatican's Congregation for Bishops, in order that the dossiers of the candidates could be examined in the ordinary way. Nor, since the Roman Commission was purely advisory, did the Pope think it necessary for the Lefebvrists to control the commission through a majority in membership. Ratzinger, aware that it would be difficult for that Episcopal review process to be completed between May 5 and June 30, obtained the Pope's permission for Lefebvre to ordain one bishop on August 15, at the close of the Marian year.

Lefebvre refused that offer. He evidently felt that Rome was angling for some way to "hem in" the Society, possibly by selecting as his successor a more moderate bishop than he himself would have chosen, possibly by out-voting the members of the Society on the Roman Commission. Despite an appeal from the Pope, a warning from the Congregation of Bishops, and a last-minute telegram from Ratzinger, Lefebvre ordained four bishops to be his successors on June 30 in Econe. Lefebvre had lived for long years on the defensive, and he remained on the defensive prior to, during, and after the signing of the May 5 protocol, as he himself later stated.

"In the case of Lefebvre," I asked, "would you do something different if you could do it again?"

"No," Ratzinger replied. "I was not able to do anything else, I must say. I really could not do anything else. No, and the Holy Father was of an openness which went to the limits in order to prevent the schism, but Lefebvre just did not have any trust."

"Was he right not to trust Rome?" I asked.

Ratzinger laughed. "That is a terrible question for a Catholic," he said. "A Catholic trusts Rome."

"But Lefebvre said he feared Rome simply wanted to slowly reform his movement and move it back into the Church and not leave it with its own identity . . . ," I replied.

"Well," Ratznger said, "his identity had to be a Catholic one, of course. As far as it possesses a closed identity, which is not compatible with the entire Catholic identity, it has to be renewed. The Church encompasses many different identities. The Jesuits have a different one compared to the Dominicans, to the Franciscans. The movements have their own identities. But, the base condition is always that the identity is not closed completely, that it is an identity within the life stream of the Church, which means in practice that it is in communion with the Pope and the bishops. We were generally willing to acknowledge a specific identity of this movement, but, of course, this identity had to open up into the life stream of the Church and overcome what hindered them truly to keep in communion with the Pope and the bishops. I think a great proposal was offered . . . I think, we really offered everything that was possible."

"And so," I asked, "when Msgr. Clemens (Cardinal Ratzinger's secretary at that time, Joseph Clemens, now a bishop) returned here on May 6 with Lefebvre's letter saying 'I must ordain the bishop on June 30,' what was your reaction?"

"Yes, it did happen like that," Ratzinger replied. "He had originally signed the agreement and had even celebrated that with Clemens in a friendly manner. And the next morning, he withdrew his signature. I was shocked, I have to say, shocked, sad and actually not completely surprised."

"Do you think of the Lefebvre affair as one of the failures of your years in office?"

"Well, I do not judge myself in terms of successes," Ratzinger said. "I think I have a clear conscience in regard to the Lefebvre matter. I did what was possible, but we were not granted reconciliation. And we certainly have to try, as far as we can, to keep the doors of reconciliation open."

"The faith of the Church comes before me"

When I asked Cardinal Ratzinger what his position was on the liturgical reform introduced after the Second Vatican Council, he insisted on a clear distinction "between the point of view of the Congregation—I don't know if there is a point of view of the Congregation—and eventual points of view that are my own personal ones. And, with regard to these last, personal points of view, one must in this matter speak with great precision. Otherwise, if one takes only a part, one creates enormous confusion . . . I would say that the essential is laid out in my book *Feast of Faith* . . . I am not and was not against the liturgical reform of the Council."

He pointed to the reforms initiated by both Pius X and Pius XII and remarked that "the liturgy in itself was in a continuous process of development, always. Because, even in the last century new feast days were introduced, others were suppressed . . . Therefore, there was a need for certain reforms, without a doubt.

"This was in harmony with the great tradition of the Latin Church. Because the Latin Church has always considered the liturgy a reality that was born in the Apostolic period and grew and developed, but that continues to grow and develop. And part of the liturgical reform, a large part, may be found simply, for example, in the increase in the choice of Prefaces. Other things—a more simple structure of the liturgical year, and also, let us say, the use of the vernacular—in principle, was a positive thing."

Then he pointed to "the dangerous side of translation." "Should the liturgy be translated also into the various dialects? Should the translations be ever more free? And must they be subjected to all the new ideas . . . ?" He insisted that the Council statements allowed "the vernacular, as is right, but the Council also said that the primary language of the liturgy is and will always be Latin." He also thought "the reforms were too brusque, even some exaggerated, not well thought out."

Ratzinger was concerned about the effect of the changes on people's faith. The legitimate new missal, he said, "does not imply that now the preceding missal is to be considered a thing entirely prohibited and excluded and negative and like a person with leprosy. . . . even from a purely sociological point of view, if a society regards something that a short time ago was the thing that was most holy, and most essential, and most to be venerated in this society, if from one day to another this venerated thing is prohibited, and comes to be considered the thing most to avoid, and most to exclude: this is the self-destruction of the society!"

Thus Ratzinger, now Pope Benedict, believes that along with the new, the old Latin liturgy "must always be protected." And he spoke of another common problem. "The continual recourse to new translations, and also the liberty granted to the priest, sometimes exaggerated, so that the liturgy appears an arbitrary thing, left to the whim of the priest and of the community, that liturgy is also destructive. Because the sense of the liturgy is precisely that the faith of the Church, which comes before me, which is not created by me, becomes present in age-old forms, not petrified but living, a reality which precedes me, which is *not* subject to arbitrary changes.

"Liturgy," Ratzinger said, "should not be the invention of the parish priest or any majority in the Church, but a gift of the Lord." And he feared "this obscuring of the *lex orandi*, (the law of prayer) because of the arbitrariness that exists, is one of the causes of the difficult situation in which the Church finds itself."

Twelve years ago, when asked, Ratzinger agreed that the Catholic Church today faces "one of the most profound crises in the history of the Church, comparable to the crisis of Gnosticism in the second and third centuries, comparable to the crisis of the Protestant Reformation, that seems clear." Now he has become Pope Benedict XVI and must lead his people through that time of crisis.

Ratzinger denies that he is a mystic. But he is drawn by the beauty and profundity of the Catholic liturgy "always penetrated by the Holy Spirit and by the presence of the Lord ... Inserting myself into this great divine fabric, I would say, becomes naturally also a profound spiritual contact of the soul with God, to feel oneself in the living presence, even a new opening of the interior eyes, to see what one could not see, and to let oneself be guided by the Lord.

"Humanity as such has always had a sense of the sacred, that is, of the untouchable, ineffable divine reality, that is, a reality entirely different from me, that is above me, that is perilous to touch, because contact with the divine is capable, in its greatness, of destroying man . . . Now we come to Christianity. The fundamental reality that God is holy and sacred also belongs to Christianity, but is totally different with regard to devotion and adoration. I would say that in Christianity, this sacred is still more defined. It coincides with this immense holiness that is God, that is, the truth, and the good, the absolute good. And . . . being absolute love, God demonstrates this love on the cross. And in this way, at the same time that he is distant, there is a new union. The believer must realize his union with Christ in the love of Christ. We have without a doubt had in the past 30 years a loss of the sacred in Christianity.

"But there has been added an additional recent factor," Ratzinger continued. "It is being argued by some now that this, the profanation of the world, this disappearance of the sacred, is precisely the intention of the New Testament. So (theology professor Johann-Baptist) Metz and others have said that the history of profanation, of de-sacralization, is the history of the victory of Christianity, because, they argue, Christianity means de-sacralization. There no longer exists this sacrality/sacredness, which is said to be something pagan and unreasonable.

"And they have interpreted, for example, the death of the

Lord outside the walls of the city, outside the sacred area, in the profanity of the world, as the explosive center of this de-sacralization. They say that the fact that the great definitive sacrifice, the liturgy of the world, is realized in the profane death of Jesus. And they say, on the other hand, that the fact that this profane death of Jesus has been understood as the true liturgy, has as a logical consequence that today there is no longer a Temple, that today there is no longer sacred and profane.

"And the way in which many have understood the liturgical reform and have carried out the liturgical reform is inspired by this idea: that, with the passing of the sacred, the liturgy *must* become radically profane, the sacred *must* disappear from the liturgy. This explains the attack on religious vestments, for example ... They see the sacred as *the* thing to transcend and the profane is the sole way to be a true Christian.

"My intention, my action is simple. I am convinced that there is a faith of the Church. The Church has formulated it in her confessions and in the documents of the magisterium. And if we want to be Catholic, we simply have to live this faith and of course unfold this faith further and further. Private opinions of this or that kind will definitely not save the Church, even if they seem to be successful at the moment.

"We have entered into the obedience of the Lord. We believe that the Lord lives in the Church and speaks in her. From this it follows simply that we need not defend private opinions, that we need not seek this or that direction, but that we try to understand what the Church really believes and that we speak up for this. Of course we have to try to make this faith understandable today and to make it alive.

We have to strive to make faith existent again in today's thinking and to show its inner logic."

The man who has now become Pope must now do with his life what he had hoped to do "in a literary way." In 1993, he said he wished for "another life span during which I could describe my theological insight." He wanted to show that Christian faith is not "some positivistic command-ment, but is to be understood, lived, acquired, and visible— that, seeing it, people can say: Yes, that is something to believe in, that is the way in which life can be lived, that is how one can find answers to the questions of life."

Last meeting

I last met with Cardinal Ratzinger on March 12, 2005, in Rome, just a month before his election as Pope Benedict XVI. It was a cold day and I was wearing an overcoat. We discussed the situation in the Ukraine, and in general the issues needing to be addressed in the dialogue with the Orthodox. We spoke of the Petrine office, and of what changes may need to occur in the way the papacy functions, to enable non-Catholics to move into closer union with Rome. And we spoke of the message of Fatima. We also discussed the liturgy at some length, the desire of many Catholics for a liturgy which is more solemn, sacred, tradi-tional, and the way to achieve that goal. We even touched on the question of Pope John Paul II's health. John Paul had just been to the hospital for a second time, and neither of us thought that he would pass away in three weeks' time.

"You know," I said to him, before I got up to leave, "our situation is filled with problems that can't be solved because they can't even be posed in clear terms."

"Yes," he replied, "as you say, we need clarity, almost more than anything, and good will."

As I took my leave and struggled a moment to put on my overcoat, he spontaneously came over to help me. It struck me then, as it does now, that it is a very kind man who extends a helping hand to a journalist.

But the hand Ratzinger is most qualified to lend has always been the hand of "clarity"—the ability to make complex and profound ideas understandable in a simple, clear way. As he once told another journalist, the most important thing for any Christian is "that we become persons who love, that is, that we realize our likeness to Christ. For, as St. John says, He is love and desires that there be creatures similar to Him who, freely choosing to love, become like Him, belong to Him and in so doing manifest His splendor."

This is Benedict XVI's intention. And it is also his cross.

Part Two

THE SPIRITUAL VISION
OF BENEDICT XVI

HIS FAITH

Having spent his entire life thinking, studying, and praying about the meaning of his Catholic faith, Benedict XVI had become one of the foremost contemporary theologians (the word literally means "Knowers of God") in the Roman Catholic Church even before his election as pope.

For Benedict XVI, God is the ultimate good, beauty, and truth, the source and fountain of all life. God is also the most profound lover of each human person, even those that do not love him, believe in him, or even know him. The most important task in life is to seek God, and to find him, and to develop a loving relationship with him, because, Benedict teaches, this leads human beings to the deepest and most lasting happiness they can experience.

Benedict XVI teaches that the eternal and invisible God appeared in this world in the form of his son, Jesus. Born in Nazareth to a particular woman whose name was Mary, he lived a human life, preached within the tradition of Jewish teachers and prophets, and died in Jerusalem 2000 years ago. This historicity, attested from many sources, means that Christianity can never be only a philosophy or a mere collection of values. Rather it must always be an encounter, a meeting with a person, a relationship of friendship and love with the very real and particular person of Jesus. Because Jesus was, and is, also uniquely divine, his life, death, and resurrection had eternal significance, altering the entire structure and meaning of our universe. This belief is the foundation of Christianity. The Holy Spirit is the continuing presence of God in the Church and world, the divine "advocate," given to humanity after Jesus himself returned to the Father. Though the divine nature is hidden, the effects of the Spirit's action are seen in the visible world. By means of the Spirit, God provides to human beings the gifts of forgiveness and the bodily healing which takes ultimate form in our resurrection from the dead.

In Mary, the woman who gave human life and birth to Jesus, human perfection was once actually present in the world—so Catholics believe. Her acceptance of God's will was so complete that she was able to give an unqualified "yes" to God's plan for her life, even when she could not understand it. That is why Christians repeat the words of the angel Gabriel in the Gospel, calling her "full of grace" and "blessed among women." Christians believe that forgiveness and life entered the world through Mary because she gave human form to the Son of God. Through Mary, as the "Second Eve" and mother of the Church, Eve's lost paradise has been regained.

As St. Paul wrote, and Benedict agrees, "all creation is in travail," and only at the end of the world will the full meaning of creation be revealed. All things in time and space have a contingent reality, moving through time from past to future, through a present moment that has no duration. Thus the created world is always dependent upon its creator. But human beings are responsible for taking care of that creation, recognizing its beauty, and filling it with goodness and love out of respect for the God who made it.

Adam (literally, the "earthling") was made from the earth, made up of physical chemicals, just as modern science believes. But "Adam" also has an aspect of being that does not come from the earth but directly from God, who "breathed into him and he became a living soul." Thus, in Benedict's teaching, human beings have a double nature: one part mortal and the other immortal. Benedict insists that the whole person must be cared for, both physically and spiritually. Christians must enter into a relationship with the eternal God, and prepare for eternal life, by doing acts of love, justice, kindness, and mercy, in this world. Theology teaches us how to do this. But the second great task of human beings is worship. The Church's liturgy, especially the Eucharist, is the means by which God's own life is transmitted to men and women, infusing them with his holiness and enabling them to bring that loving holiness into the world.

The Church's liturgy and teaching, however, are founded upon God's original Covenant with the "Chosen People," the Jews. Benedict XVI sees the emergence in human history of the Jewish people not simply as a sociological development but as part of God's plan for the whole human race. Thus, the significance of Abraham's call, of Isaac and Jacob and the 12 tribes of Israel, and of the prophets, remains profoundly important. The Jews were, and are, "a light to the nations." Christians believe, however, that the coming of Jesus Christ, born into the Jewish family of Joseph and Mary, was at once a continuation and a fulfillment of that history, extending God's Covenant to the whole world.

The Church, "catholic" in its universality, is, for Pope

Benedict, the continuation in the world of the community of believers Jesus himself first gathered. The Church and her members must therefore act as Jesus acted, preaching the word of God, comforting the sick, forgiving sinners, and communicating Jesus' life to others through the mystery of the Eucharist. As the "Bride of Christ," the communal yet personal human society which Christ loves and is faithful to until the end, the Church transcends political and sociological analysis. As the "mystical body of Christ," the Church is, mystically but truly, Jesus alive in the world, from the first Easter until the end of time.

The Church's sacraments are "visible signs of an invisible reality," which Catholics consider a "means of grace," ways of receiving God's spirit into one's being in order to become the people God wants us to be. In Catholicism, there are seven sacraments: Baptism, Penance and Reconciliation, The Eucharist, Confirmation, Matrimony, Holy Orders, and Anointing of the Sick. Baptism initiates one into the life of Christ. Penance and Reconciliation provides forgiveness and spiritual rebirth. The Eucharist enables Christians to be united with the living body and blood of Jesus. Confirmation involves a mature commitment of faith which brings spiritual gifts. Matrimony is a sacrament administered by a man and a women to each other for a lifetime unity in marriage. Holy Orders prepares those who are ordained for a life of service to Jesus and God's people. Anointing the Sick provides healing grace to the seriously ill or prepares the dying soul for its final journey.

Pope Benedict, like St. Paul, believes that "all men seek God and grope toward him." He respects this innate longing for the divine and the eternal, and recognizes that God can and will grant salvation to all who seek for truth. Christians believe that the true fulfillment of all human longing, and ultimate spiritual blessedness, is to be found in the God revealed by Jesus Christ, who came as a "Good Shepherd," to save all people, even those "lost sheep" who have wandered far. Benedict XVI, following in Christ's footsteps, wishes to be in respectful dialogue with all other faiths, practicing Christ's love in action and sharing the joy of his own faith with the entire world.

I

THE QUESTION

What is the path?

Each human life is an open question, an incomplete, not fully realized project, something to be brought to fruition. Each human being faces these questions: how can the full potential of my life be realized? How does one learn the art of living? What is the path to true happiness?

Is the universe absurd, or not?

Is the world to be understood as originating from a creative intellect, or as arising out of a combination of probabilities in the realm of the absurd? Today as yesterday, this alternative is the decisive question for our comprehension of reality; it cannot be dodged.

The deepest poverty

To evangelize means: to reveal the path to true happiness— to teach the art of complete living. At the beginning of his public life Jesus says: I have come to evangelize the poor

(Luke 4:18). This means, "I have come to respond to the fundamental question of your existence. I am here to show you the path of life, the path to happiness. I am, in fact, that path."

The deepest poverty is not material poverty but spiritual poverty: the inability to be joyful, the conviction that life is absurd and contradictory. In different forms this poverty is widespread today, both in the materially rich and in the impoverished nations.

The inability to love

The inability to grasp joy comes from and leads to the inability to love ... When the art of living remains unknown, nothing else functions rightly.

The grain of mustard seed

Large things always begin from the small seed ... In other words: the great realities begin in humility. This truth is seen in the very actions of God in history: "The Lord did not set his affection on you and choose you because you were more numerous than other peoples, for you were the fewest of all peoples. But it was because the Lord loved you." God says this to the People of Israel in the Old Testament and thus expresses the fundamental paradox of the history of salvation—that God does not count in large numbers. Exterior power is not the sign of his presence. Most of Jesus' parables describe this structure in divine intervention, and thus address the disciples' natural concerns and expectations about other kinds of success and signs from the Messiah—the kinds of success that are offered by Satan to the Lord: "All these—the kingdoms of the world—I will give to you ..." (Matthew 4:9). An old proverb says: "Success is not one of the names of God." The new evangelization must surrender to the mystery of the grain of mustard seed . . .

A paradox

In the history of salvation, it is always Good Friday and Easter Sunday at the same time.

"By night he prayed"

A few years ago, I was reading the biography of a very good priest of our century, Don Didimo, the parish priest of Bassano del Grappa. In his notes, golden words can be found, the fruit of a life of prayer and of meditation. Don Didimo says: "Jesus preached by day, by night he prayed." With these few words, he wished to say: Jesus had to acquire the disciples from God. This is always true.

We ourselves cannot gather men. We must acquire them by God for God. All methods are empty without the foundation of prayer. The word of proclamation must always be drenched in an intense life of prayer.

The seed that dies

Jesus preached by day, by night he prayed—this is not all. His entire life was—as demonstrated in a beautiful way by the Gospel according to St. Luke—a path toward the cross, a going up toward Jerusalem. Jesus did not redeem the world with beautiful words but with his suffering and his death . . . The Lord himself—extending and amplifying the parable of the grain of mustard seed—formulated this law of fruitfulness in the parable of the grain of seed that dies, fallen to earth (John 12:24). This law too is valid until the end of the world . . .

Each birth requires suffering

Throughout all periods of history, the words of Tertullian have always been verified: The blood of martyrs is a seed. St. Augustine comments on the text John 21:16 in the following way: " 'Tend my sheep'—this means suffer for my sheep . . . A mother cannot give life to a child without suffering. Each birth requires suffering, is suffering, and becoming a Christian is a birth." We cannot give life to others without giving up our own lives . . . And let us think about the words of the Savior: "Whoever loses his life for my sake and the Gospel's will save it" (Mark 8:35).

"Repent and believe"

The fundamental content of the Old Testament is summarized in the message by John the Baptist: metanoeìte—Convert! There is no access to Jesus without the Baptist; there is no possibility of reaching Jesus without answering the call of the precursor, rather: Jesus took up the message of John in the synthesis of his own preaching: *metanoeìte kaì pisteúete èn tù eùaggelíu* (Mark 1:15, "repent and believe in the Gospel").

The Greek word *"metanoeìte"* means to rethink—to question one's normal and ordinary way of living; to allow God to enter into the value system of one's life, to not merely judge according to the current opinions. Thus, to convert means not to live as all the others live, not to do what everyone else does, not to feel justified in dubious, ambiguous, evil actions just because others do, to begin to see one's life through the eyes of God; thereby looking for the good, even if uncomfortable; not to depend on the judgment of the majority, but on the justice of God—in other words, to look for a new style of life, a new life.

The "I" and the "You"

We must bear in mind the social aspect of conversion. Certainly, conversion is above all a very personal act, intensely personal. I separate myself from the formula "to live as everyone else does." I find my own person in front of God, my own personal responsibility.

But true personalization is always also a new and more profound socialization. The "I" opens itself once again to the "you," in all its depths, and thus a new "We" is born.

If the lifestyle spread throughout the world implies the danger of depersonalization, of not living one's own life but the life of all the others, in conversion a new "We," of the common path of God, must be achieved. In proclaiming conversion we must also offer a community of life, a common space for the new style of life. We cannot evangelize with words alone; the Gospel creates life, creates communities of progress; a merely individual conversion has no consistency ...

The Kingdom of God Is God

The key phrase of the proclamation of Jesus is: the Kingdom of God. But the Kingdom of God is not a thing, a social or political structure, a utopia. The Kingdom of God is God. The Kingdom of God means: God exists. God is alive. God is present and acts in the world, in our—in my—life. God is not a faraway "ultimate cause," God is not the "great architect" of deism, who created the machine of the world and is no longer part of it. On the contrary: God is the most present and decisive reality in each and every act of my life, in each and every moment of history.

The absence of God

The true problem of our times is the "Crisis of God," the absence of God, disguised by an empty religiosity. Theology must go back to being truly "theo-logy," speaking about and with God. The one necessity *(unum necessarium)* of man is God. Everything changes, whether God exists or not. Unfortunately, we Christians also often live as if God did not exist *("si Deus non daretur")*. We often live according to the slogan: "God does not exist, and if he exists, he does not belong." Therefore, evangelization must, first of all, speak about God, proclaim the only true God: the Creator—the Sanctifier—the Judge.

II

GOD

A day of God's absence

Holy Saturday, the day of the burial of God—is that not in an uncanny way our day? Does our century not begin to become one large Holy Saturday, a day of God's absence?

The essence of religion

The essence of religion is the relation of man beyond himself to the unknown reality that faith calls God. It is man's capacity to go beyond all tangible, measurable reality and to enter into this primordial relation.

Getting to know God . . . through prayer

God cannot be made known with words alone. One does not really know a person if one knows about this person only from others. To proclaim God is to introduce the relation with God—to instruct how to pray. Prayer is faith in action. And only by experiencing life with God does the evidence of his existence appear. This is why schools of prayer, communities of prayer, are so important. There is a complementarity between personal prayer ("in one's room," alone in front of God's eyes), "para-liturgical" prayer in common ("popular religiosity"), and liturgical prayer.

The liturgy as prayer

The liturgy is, first of all, prayer; its primary object is not ourselves (as in private prayer and in popular religiosity), but God himself. The liturgy is *actio divina* ("divine action"): God acts and we respond to this divine action. Speaking about God and speaking with God must always go together. The liturgy (the sacraments) are not a secondary theme next to the preaching about the living God, but the realization of our relationship with God.

Should we be afraid of God?

I am not afraid of God because God is good. Naturally, I recognize my weaknesses, my sins and know these can wound the Lord who cares for us so deeply. I suppose that in this sense I'm afraid of how my actions will affect God—something quite different from the traditional understanding of fear. In this sense, I am not afraid of God; I revere the Lord and so I wouldn't want to do anything that would harm him.

The authentic adoration of God

The ancient Church rightly understood the word "orthodoxy" not to mean "right doctrine" but to mean the authentic adoration and glorification of God. They were convinced that everything depended on being in the right relationship with God, on knowing what pleases him and what one can do to respond to him in the right way. For this reason, Israel loved the law: from it, they knew how to live righteously and how to honor God in the right way: by acting in accord with his will, bringing order into the world, opening it to the transcendent.

This was the new joy Christians discovered: that now, beginning with Christ, they understood how God ought to be glorified and how, precisely through this, the world would become just.

That these two things should go together—how God is glorified and how justice comes—the angels had proclaimed on the holy night: "Glory to God in the highest, and peace on earth, goodwill toward men," they had said (Luke 2:14).

God's power

A powerless God is a contradiction in terms. If he cannot act, cannot speak, and be spoken to . . . he has nothing to do with what the religious belief of mankind means by "God."

"Like an arrow in flight"

Worship means accepting that our life is like an arrow in flight. Accepting that nothing finite can be my goal or determine the direction of my life, but that I myself must pass by all possible goals. That is, to pass beyond them into being inwardly at one with him who wished me to exist as a partner in relationship with him and who has given me freedom precisely in this.

God's guidance

God speaks quietly. But he gives us all kinds of signs. In retrospect, especially, we can see that he has given us a little nudge through a friend, through a book, or through what we see as a failure—even through accidents. Life is actually full of these silent indications. If I remain alert then slowly ... I begin to feel how God is guiding me.

Testing God

There is in Deuteronomy an allusion to the episode in which Israel risks dying of thirst in the desert. There was a rebellion against Moses, which became a rebellion against God. God must show that he is God.

This rebellion against God is described like this in the Bible: "They put the Lord to the test, saying: 'Is the Lord in the midst of us, yes or no?'" (Exodus 17:7) ... God must submit himself to a test. He is "tested" just as merchandise is tested. He must submit to conditions that we declare are necessary for our certainty. If he does not now guarantee the protection promised in Psalm 90, then he is not God. In this case, he would have been false to his own word and thus to himself.

We find ourselves here faced with the whole great problem of how we can know and how we cannot know God, of how man can be in relationship with God and of how he can lose him. The human presumption that would reduce God to an object and impose upon him our scientific conditions, cannot find God. In fact, this presupposes already that we deny God as God, because we place ourselves above him. Because if we do this, we set aside the whole dimension of love, of interior listening, and recognize as real only that which can be tested, only that which is given into our hands.

Who thinks in this way renders himself God and so degrades not only God, but the world and himself.

God's sense of humor

Humor is . . . an essential element in the mirth of creation. We can see how, in many matters in our lives, God wants to prod us into taking things a bit more lightly, to see the funny side of it, to get down off our pedestal and not forget our sense of fun.

God is ultimately faithful

He who follows the will of God knows that in the middle of all the horrors he may encounter he will not lose the ultimate protection. He knows that the foundation of the world is love and that therefore even where no man can or will help him he can go forward trusting in him, who loves him. This trust which the Scripture authorizes us to have and to which the Lord, the Resurrected One, invites us, is however something totally other than the risky provocation of God, which would make God into our servant.

God's greatness

Being reasonable, one would have to say that God is far too great for one idea or a single book to comprehend his whole word. Only in many experiences, even contradictory experiences, can he give us reflections of himself.

God's glory inseparable from peace on earth

God's glory and peace on earth are inseparable. Where God is excluded, there is a breakdown of peace in the world; without God, no *orthopraxis* (action) can save us. In fact, there does not exist an *orthopraxis* which is simply just, detached from a knowledge of what is good. The will without knowledge is blind, and so action, *orthopraxis*, is blind without knowledge and leads into the abyss. Marxism's great deception was to tell us that we had long enough reflected on the world, that now it was at last time to change it. But if we do not know in what direction to change it, if we do not understand its meaning and its inner purpose, change for change's sake alone becomes destruction—as we have seen and continue to see. But the inverse is also true: doctrine alone, which does not become life and action, becomes idle chatter and in this way becomes equally empty. The truth is concrete. Knowledge and action are closely united, as faith and life are linked.

III

JESUS CHRIST

The historical Jesus

Today, the temptation is great to diminish Jesus Christ, the Son of God, into a merely historical Jesus, into a pure man. One does not necessarily deny the divinity of Jesus, but by using certain methods one distills from the Bible a Jesus reduced to our size, a Jesus possible and comprehensible within the parameters of our historiography.

But this "historical Jesus" is an artifact, the image of his authors rather than the image of the living God. The Christ of faith is not a myth; the so-called historical Jesus is a mythological figure, self-invented by various interpreters.

A central truth

It must be firmly believed as a truth of Catholic faith that the universal salvific will of the One and Triune God is offered and accomplished once and for all in the mystery of the incarnation, death, and resurrection of the Son of God.

The heart's longing

Christ is the Love of God made flesh, the Only Son and Savior of all. For you, to proclaim Christ is not to impose something foreign on anyone but to communicate to all what each one basically longs for: the eternal love that every human heart is secretly awaiting.

The heart of Jesus

In the Heart of Jesus, the center of Christianity is set before us. It expresses everything, all that is genuinely new and revolutionary in the New Covenant. This Heart calls to our heart. It invites us to step forth out of the futile attempt of self-preservation and, by joining in the task of love, by handing ourselves over to him and with him, to discover the fullness of love which alone is eternity and which alone sustains the world.

Why we say "before Christ" and "after Christ"

The secular regimes, which do not want to speak about Christ and, on the other hand, do not want to ignore altogether the western calculation of time, substitute the words "before the birth of Christ" and "after the birth of Christ" with formulas like "before and after the common era," or similar phrases. But does this not rather deepen the question: what happened at that moment that made it the change of an era? What was there in that moment that meant a new historical age was beginning, so that time for us begins anew from that date? Why do we no longer measure time from the foundation of Rome, from the Olympiads, from the years of a sovereign or even from the creation of the world? Does this beginning of 2,000 years ago still have any importance for us? Does it have a foundational dimension? What does it say to us? Or has this beginning become for us something empty of meaning, a mere technical convention which we conserve for purely pragmatic reasons? But what then orients our joy? Is it like a vessel that in fact has no course and is now simply pursuing its voyage in the hope that somewhere there may exist an end?

The essential

What is essential about Christ is not that he proclaimed certain ideas . . . Rather I become a Christian by believing in this event. God stepped into the World and acted; so it is an action, a reality, not only an intellectual entity.

"To see" Jesus

After all, the sole and sufficient purpose . . . is to see Jesus . . . [to] contemplate him in his inexhaustible words, contemplate him in his mysteries—as Saint Ignatius provides in his Spiritual Exercises—the nativity mysteries, the mystery of his hidden life, the mystery of the public life, the paschal mystery, the sacraments, the history of the Church. The Rosary and the Stations of the Cross are nothing else than a guide devised by the heart of the Church to learn to "see Jesus" and thus to arrive of Nineveh—repentance, conversion. The Rosary and the Stations of the Cross have been for centuries the great school for seeing Jesus.

These days invite us to enter this school again, in common with the faithful of so many centuries.

A love story

Only Christ gives meaning to the whole of our life... Christianity is not an intellectual system, a packet of dogmas, a moralism. Christianity is rather an encounter, a love story; it is an event. This love affair with Christ, this love story which is the whole of his life was however far from every superficial enthusiasm, from every vague romanticism. Really seeing Christ, he [Don Luigi Giussani, founder of the Catholic "Communion and Liberation" movement in Italy] knew that to encounter Christ means to follow Christ. This encounter is a road, a journey, a journey that passes also—as we heard in the psalm—through the "valley of darkness." In the Gospel, we heard of the last darkness of Christ's suffering, of the apparent absence of God, when the world's Sun was eclipsed. He knew that to follow is to pass through a "valley of darkness," to take the way of the cross, and to live all the same in true joy.

Knowledge of the beauty of Christ

Being struck and overcome by the beauty of Christ is a more real, more profound knowledge than mere rational deduction. Of course we must not underrate the importance of theological reflection, of exact and precise theological thought; it remains absolutely necessary. But to move from here to disdain or to reject the impact produced by the response of the heart in the encounter with beauty as a true form of knowledge would impoverish us and dry up our faith and our theology. We must rediscover this form of knowledge; it is a pressing need of our time.

The beauty of the King

Psalm 44 describes the wedding of the King, his beauty, his virtues, his mission, and then becomes an exaltation of his bride . . . The third verse of Psalm 44 says: "You are the fairest of the children of men and grace is poured upon your lips." Naturally, the Church reads this psalm as a poetic-prophetic representation of Christ's spousal relationship with his Church. She recognizes Christ as the fairest of men, the grace poured upon his lips points to the inner beauty of his words, the glory of his proclamation.

So it is not merely the external beauty of the Redeemer's appearance that is glorified: rather, the beauty of Truth appears in him, the beauty of God himself who draws us to himself and, at the same time captures us with the wound of Love, the holy passion (eros), that enables us to go forth together, with and in the Church his Bride, to meet the Love who calls us.

On Monday of Holy Week, however, the Church changes the antiphon and invites us to interpret Psalm 44 in the light of Is 53:2: "He had neither beauty, no majesty, nothing to attract our eyes, no grace to make us delight in him." How can we reconcile this? The appearance of the "fairest of the children of men" is so wretched that no one desires to look at him. Pilate presented him to the crowd saying: "Behold the man!" to rouse sympathy for the crushed and battered Man, in whom no external beauty remained.

"The Beautiful will save us."

Is there anyone who does not know Dostoyevsky's often quoted sentence: "The Beautiful will save us"? However, people usually forget that Dostoyevsky is referring here to the redeeming Beauty of Christ. We must learn to see him.

If we know him, not only in words, but if we are struck by the arrow of his paradoxical beauty, then we will truly know him, and know him not only because we have heard others speak about him. Then we will have found the beauty of Truth, of the Truth that redeems.

Nothing can bring us into close contact with the beauty of Christ himself other than the world of beauty created by faith and light that shines out from the faces of the saints, through whom his own light becomes visible.

The temptations of Jesus

The account of the temptations follows the narration of the baptism of Jesus, in which the mystery of the death of the resurrection, of sin and of redemption, of sin and of forgiveness, are prefigured: Jesus descends into the depths of the Jordan. To be immersed in the river is a moment of death represented symbolically. An old life is buried, so that the new may arise. Since Jesus himself is without sin, he has no old life to bury, and so the acceptance of baptism is an anticipation of the cross, and the entrance into our destiny, the acceptance of our sins, and of our death. At the moment he emerges again, the heavens are opened and from them resounds the voice with which the Father recognizes him as his son. The open heavens are a sign indicating that this descent into our night opens the new day and through this identification of the Son with us the wall between God and man is breached: God is no longer inaccessible; in the profundity of death and of our sins, he seeks us out and bears us anew into the light. In this sense, the baptism of Jesus anticipates the entire drama of his life and death and at the same time enables us to comprehend it.

His suffering

Jesus, whose divine love alone can redeem all humanity, wants us to share his Cross so that we can complete what is still lacking in his suffering (cf. Col 1:24). Whenever we show kindness to the suffering, the persecuted, and defenseless, and share in their sufferings, we help to carry that same Cross of Jesus. In this way we obtain salvation and help contribute to the salvation of the world.

The face on the cloth

"Your face, Lord, do I seek. Hide not your face from me" (Ps 27:8-9). Veronica—Bernice, in the Greek tradition—embodies the universal yearning of the devout men and women of the Old Testament, the yearning of all believers to see the face of God. On Jesus' Way of the Cross, though, she at first did nothing more than perform an act of womanly kindness: she held out a facecloth to Jesus. She did not let herself be deterred by the brutality of the soldiers or the fear which gripped the disciples. She is the image of that good woman, who, amid turmoil and dismay, shows the courage born of goodness and does not allow her heart to be bewildered.

"In the light of Christ"

Christ is totally different from all the founders of other religions, and he cannot be reduced to a Buddha, a Socrates, or a Confucius. He is really the bridge between heaven and earth, the light of truth who has appeared to us. The gift of knowing Jesus does not mean that there are no important fragments of truth in other religions. In the light of Christ, we can establish a fruitful dialogue . . . in which we can see how all these fragments of truth contribute to greater depth

in our faith and to an authentic spiritual community of humanity . . . I would say that at the present time the dialogue
with the other religions is the most important point: to understand how, on one hand, Christ is unique, and on the
other, how he answers all others, who are precursors of
Christ, and who are in dialogue with Christ.

⚜ IV ⚜

THE HOLY SPIRIT

A prolongation of the story

The third section of the Creed refers in the first place
not to the Holy Ghost as the third person in the Godhead
but to the Holy Spirit as God's gift to history in the community of those who believe in Christ . . . The third section
was bound to be understood as a prolongation of the story
of Christ in the gift of the Spirit, and therefore as a reference to the "last days" between the coming of Christ and
his return. It speaks, as we have already seen, not of God's
inner life but of "God facing outward," of the Holy Spirit
as the power through which the risen Lord remains present
in the history and a new world. This tendency produced of
its own accord a further consequence. The fact that it is a
question here not of the Spirit as a person within God but
as the power of God in the history that opens with the resurrection of Jesus produced the effect that in the consciousness of those praying faith in the "Spirit" and faith in the
Church interacted with each other.

Christ remains present

Christ remains present through the Holy Spirit with all his openness and breadth and freedom, which by no means excludes the institutional form but limits its claims and does not allow it simply to make itself the same as worldly institutions.

The work of the Spirit—Revelation

In Christ, God has said everything—that is, he has revealed himself completely—and therefore Revelation came to an end with the fulfillment of the mystery of Christ as enunciated in the New Testament.

What is revelation?

If revelation is understood as a series of supernatural communications which took place in the time of Jesus' activity and were definitively closed with the death of the apostles, then the faith, practically speaking, is to be understood only as a connection with a construction of thought built in the past. But this historicizing and intellectualizing concept of revelation, which has become ever more developed in the modern epoch, is simply false. In fact, revelation is not a series of affirmations—the revelation is Christ himself; he is the Logos, the Word which embraces everything, in which God himself expresses himself and therefore whom we call Son of God. This unique Logos naturally expressed himself in everyday words, in which he shows us who he is. But the Word is always greater than words and is never fully expressed in words.

The Spirit today

In the heart of a world desiccated by rationalistic skepticism, a new experience of the Holy Spirit has come about,

amounting to a worldwide renewal movement. What the New
Testament describes with reference to the charisms as visible
signs of the coming of the Spirit is no longer merely ancient,
past history: this history is becoming a burning reality today.

V

MARY

What was Mary like?

In Luke, Mary stands as the embodiment of the Church's
memory ... Thus Mary becomes a model for the Church's
mission, i.e., that of being a dwelling place for the Word,
preserving it and keeping it safe in times of confusion, protecting it, as it were, from the elements.

"A human being with depth"

She is also the interpretation of the parable of the seed
sowed in good soil and yielding fruit a hundredfold ... She
is a human being with depth. She lets the word sink deep
into her. So the process of fruitful transformation can take
place in a twofold direction: she saturated the Word with
her life, as it were, putting the sap and energy of her life at
the Word's disposal; but as a result, conversely, her life is
permeated, enriched, and deepened by the energies of the
Word, which gives everything its meaning.

Mary's "fiat" (Her response to the angel at the Annunciation)

The "fiat" ("let it be done") of Mary, the word of her
heart, has changed the history of the world, because it
brought the Savior into the world.

"Daughter of Zion"

As the true "Daughter of Zion," Mary is the image of the Church, the image of believing man who can only come to salvation and to himself through the gift of love—through grace.

Mary's courage

It was said to Mary: "And behold, you will conceive in your womb and bear a son. He will be great and the Lord God will give to him the throne of his father David" (Lk 1:31ff.). And she would hear from the mouth of the elderly Simeon: "A sword will pierce through your own soul" (Lk 2:35). She would then recall the words of the prophets, words like these: "He was oppressed, and he was afflicted, yet he opened not his mouth; he was like a lamb that is led to slaughter" (Is 53:7). Now it all takes place. In her heart she had kept the words of the angel, spoken to her in the beginning: "Do not be afraid, Mary" (Lk 1:30). The disciples fled, yet she did not flee. She stayed there, with a Mother's courage, a Mother's fidelity, a Mother's goodness, and a faith which did not waver in the hour of darkness: "Blessed is she who believed" (Lk 1:45).

"Back to Mary"

If the place occupied by Mary has been essential to the equilibrium of the faith, today it is urgent, as in few other epochs of Church history, to rediscover that place. It is necessary to go back to Mary if we want to return to that "truth about Jesus Christ," "truth about the Church" and the "truth about man."

Prayer to Mary

Holy Mary, Mother of the Lord, you remained faithful when the disciples fled. Just as you believed the angels' incredible message—that you would become the Mother of

the Most High, so too you believed at the hour of his greatest abasement. In this way, at the hour of the Cross, at the
hour of the world's darkest night, you became the Mother
of all believers, the Mother of the Church. We beg you:
teach us to believe, and grant that our faith may bear fruit
in courageous service and be the sign of a love ever ready to
share suffering and to offer assistance.

❧ VI ❧

CREATION

Creation—An expression of love

There is nothing degrading about dependence when it
takes the form of love, for then it is no longer dependence,
the diminishing of self through competition with others.
Dependence in the form of love precisely constitutes the self
as self and sets it free, because love essentially takes the form
of saying, "I want you to be." It is creativity, the only creative
power, which can bring forth the other as other without envy
or loss of self.

❧ VII ❧

HUMANITY

"Heaven and earth touch"

In the human being heaven and earth touch one another.
In the human being God enters into his creation; the human
being is directly related to God. . . . Each human being is

known by God and loved by him. Each is willed by God, and each is God's image. Precisely in this consists the deeper and greater unity of humankind—that each of us, each individual human being, realizes the *one* project of God and has his or her origin in the same creative idea of God.

Today

Today we look for something religious, something religious that gives us a certain degree of satisfaction. Humanity wants to understand the infinite, to have the answers about that other dimension, that "other side" that exudes the sweetness and hope that material things cannot give. I really think this is a big trend today: separating yourself from the need of faith, from a concrete "yes" to God that is full of meaning. People are looking more for immediate satisfaction without the need to truly commit themselves. While it can be very nice to enter into this mystical dimension—without any commitment—you end up merely satisfying immediate wants and you are imprisoned in your sense of self.

A being capable of prayer

The value of each human life, in the perspective of the "Gospel of life," derives from its being the "image" of God, from its having, in its "likeness" to the Creator, a tendency to place itself in relationship with him. Yes, man is truly great precisely because he is "capable of God," because he is called to enter into a relationship with God and to call him "You." Yes, to the question: "What precisely distinguishes man from the animals and why does human life merit such an absolute respect?" one must answer: man is the being capable of thinking about God, he is the being capable of prayer.

Members of the Body of Christ

We must always see in other human beings persons with whom we shall one day share God's joy. We must look upon them as persons who are called, together with us, to be members of the Body of Christ, with whom we shall one day sit at table with Abraham, Isaac, and Jacob, and with Christ himself, as their brothers and sisters, as the brothers and sisters of Christ, and as the children of God.

The arrogance of man

The arrogance that makes us think that we ourselves can create human beings has turned man into a kind of merchandise, to be bought and sold, or stored to provide parts for experimentation. In doing this, we hope to conquer death by our own efforts, yet in reality we are profoundly debasing human dignity. Lord help us; we have fallen. Help us to abandon our destructive pride and, by learning from your humility, to rise again.

The core of the mystery: Humility

This, then, is the question: Are we truly watchful? Are we free; are we adaptable? Are we not, all of us, suffering from snobbishness, from an arrogant skepticism? How can a person hear the voice of an angel if he is convinced in advance that there are no angels? Even if he were to hear it, he would have to interpret it in his own way. And what of the individual who is accustomed always to set himself up as judge? I realize more and more why Saint Augustine regarded "humilitas," humility, as the core of Christ's mystery.

"Above the waters of time"

Are we not so submerged, from one day to the next, from one task to the next, in the details of daily living, in its endless demands and difficulties, that we have no time even for ourselves? If that is so, then this should be the hour when we rise above these things, the hour when we try for a moment to see the heavens above the waters and the stars that shine upon us, in order, at the same time, to comprehend ourselves. We should try to review and evaluate the way we have traveled. We should try to see where we have gone wrong, what has obstructed for us the way that leads to ourselves and to others.

"Man has fallen"

Man has fallen, and he continues to fall. Often he becomes a caricature of himself, no longer the image of God, but a mockery of the Creator. Is not the man who, on the way from Jerusalem to Jericho, fell among robbers who stripped him and left him half-dead and bleeding beside the road, the image of humanity par excellence? Jesus' fall beneath the Cross is not just the fall of the man Jesus, exhausted from his scourging. There is a more profound meaning in this fall, as Paul tells us in the Letter to the Philippians: "though he was in the form of God, he did not count equality with God a thing to be grasped, but emptied himself, taking the form of a servant, being born in the likeness of men ... He humbled himself and became obedient unto death, even death on a Cross" (Phil 2:6-8).

Jesus does not fall

Analogically, the account of the temptations is an anticipation, a mirror of the mystery of God and of man, of the mystery of Jesus Christ. In the account, Jesus continues the descent that he initiated in the moment of incarnation, made visible publicly in the baptism, which will lead him to the cross and the tomb, to Sheol, the world of the dead. But in the account there is also accomplished a new ascent, which opens and renders possible the ascent of man from his abyss and beyond himself. The 40 days of Christ's fast in the desert recall above all the 40 days that Moses passed in fasting on Mt. Sinai, before he could receive the Word of God, the sacred tablets of covenant. They can also recall the rabbinical account wherein Abraham during his journey to Mt. Horeb took neither food nor drink for 40 days and 40 nights and nourished himself on the sight and word of the angel that accompanied him. They remind us also of Israel's 40 years in the desert, which were the time of Israel's testing as well as the time of a particular closeness to God. The Fathers also saw in the number 40 the symbolic number of the time of human history and so also considered the 40 days of Jesus in the desert as the image of every human life. The temptations of Jesus could thus in the end even be understood as the repetition and overcoming of the original temptation of Adam. In fact: the Letter to the Hebrews strongly emphasizes that Jesus is able to be compassionate with us, because he himself was tried in every way, like us, excluding, of course, sin (Hebrews 2:18; 4:15). His being tempted was an essential part of his being human, of his descent into communion with us, in the abyss of our misery.

✦ VIII ✦

JUDAISM

"Already as a child"

Already as a child, I could not understand how some people wanted to derive a condemnation of Jews from the death of Jesus, because the following thought had penetrated my soul as something profoundly consoling: Jesus' blood raises no call for retaliation but calls all to reconciliation. It has become as the letter to the Hebrews shows, itself a permanent day of atonement to God.

Jews and Christians should accept each other in profound inner reconciliation, neither in disregard of their faith nor in its denial. But out of the depth of faith itself. In their mutual reconciliation they should become a force for peace in and for the world. Through their witness through the one God, who cannot be adored apart from the unity of love, of God and neighbor, they should open the door into the world for this God so that his will be done and so that it becomes on earth "as it is in heaven"; so that "his kingdom come."

"Two things are very clear"

Two things are very clear in the Holy Scripture. In the Letter of St. Paul to the Romans, he clearly says, "The fidelity of God is absolutely clear. He is faithful to His promises." And so, the people of Abraham are always God's people, on the one hand. And he says also clearly, "All Israel will be saved." But, it is also clear that Jesus is the Savior, not only of the other peoples, he is a Jew and he is the Savior, especially of his own people. St. Bernard of Clairvaux said, "God saved, reserved for himself, the salvation of Israel. He will do it in His Own Person." And so, we have to leave it to God's Self, to see, convinced and knowing, that Christ is Savior of all of His Own people, and of all people. But how He will do it is in God's Hand.

⚜ IX ⚜

THE CHURCH

Tiny lights in the darkness of history

Following Christ means loving his Church, his Mystical Body. By moving in this direction we light tiny lights in this world, we dispel the darkness of history.

Why the Church should not be "trendy"

In an interview in 1975, Eugene Ionesco, one of the founders of the theater of the absurd, expressed the passion of seeking and searching that characterizes the person of our age. I quote here a few sentences from that interview: "The Church does not want to lose her present clientele; but she does want to gain new members. The result is a kind of secularization that is truly pitiful. The world is losing its way; the Church is losing herself in the world . . . I once heard a priest say in Church: Let us be happy; let us shake hands . . . Jesus is pleased to wish you a pleasant 'good day'! Before long they will be setting up a bar in church for the Communion of bread and wine and offering sandwiches and Beaujolais . . . Nothing is left to us; nothing is solid. Everything is in flux. But what we need is a rock." It seems to me that if we listen to the voices of our age, of people who are consciously living, suffering, and loving in the world today, we will realize that we cannot serve this world with a kind of banal officiousness. It has no need of confirmation but rather of transformation, of the radicalism of the Gospel.

The Church's temptation to take political power.

The Christian Roman Empire sought very early on to make of the faith a political factor in the unity of the empire. The kingdom of Christ was to have assumed the configuration of a political kingdom, and of such a kingdom's splendor. The weakness of the faith, the earthly fragility of Jesus Christ, were to be sustained by a political or military power. Down through the centuries, this temptation to ensure the faith's survival by power has re-emerged in many different forms, and always the faith has been threatened with suffocation in the embrace of power. The struggle for the freedom of the Church, the struggle so that the kingdom of Jesus not be assimilated into any political form, must be carried out in every century. In fact, the price of faith's union with political power is always paid in the end when faith is placed at the service of power and must bow to its criteria.

On becoming supreme pontiff of the church

Surprising every prevision I had, Divine Providence, through the will of the venerable Cardinal Fathers, called me to succeed this great Pope. I have been thinking in these hours about what happened in the region of Caesarea Philippi two thousand years ago: I seem to hear the words of Peter: "You are Christ, the Son of the living God," and the solemn affirmation of the Lord: "You are Peter and on this rock I will build my Church ... I will give you the keys of the kingdom of heaven."

You are Christ! You are Peter! It seems I am reliving this very Gospel scene; I, the successor of Peter, repeat with trepidation the anxious words of the fisherman from Galilee and I listen again with intimate emotion to the re-assuring promise of the divine Master. If the weight of the responsibility that now lies on my poor shoulders is enor-mous, the divine power on which I can count is surely im-measurable: "You are Peter and on this rock I will build my Church." Electing me as the Bishop of Rome, the Lord wanted me as his Vicar, he wished me to be the "rock" upon which everyone may rest with confidence. I ask him to make up for the poverty of my strength, that I may be a coura-geous and faithful pastor of his flock, always docile to the inspirations of his spirit.

On his sentiments as the Pope

Grace and peace in abundance to all of you! In my soul there are two contrasting sentiments in these hours. On the one hand, a sense of inadequacy and human turmoil for the responsibility entrusted to me yesterday as the Successor of the Apostle Peter in this See of Rome, with regard to the Universal Church. On the other hand I sense within me profound gratitude to God who—as the liturgy makes us sing—does not abandon his flock, but leads it throughout time, under the guidance of those whom he has chosen as vicars of his Son, and made pastors.

🕭 X 🕭

THE SACRAMENTS

Anticipation of the new world

Israel was journeying to the Promised Land. The whole of humanity is seeking something like the Promised Land. The Easter liturgy is very specific on this point. Its goals are the sacraments of Christian initiation: Baptism, Confirmation, the Holy Eucharist. The Church thus tells us that these sacraments are the anticipation of the new world, its presence anticipated in our lives.

Baptism—a new life

In the ancient Church the Catechumenate was a journey step by step to Baptism: a journey of the opening of the senses, heart, and mind to God, the learning of a new lifestyle, a transformation of personal existence into growing friendship with Christ in the company of all believers.

Thus, after the various stages of purification, openness, and new awareness, the sacramental act of Baptism was the definitive gift of new life. It was a death and resurrection, as St. Paul says in a sort of spiritual autobiography: *"I have been crucified with Christ; it is no longer I who live, but Christ who lives in me, and the life I now live in the flesh I live by faith in the Son of God, who loved me and gave himself for me"* (Gal 2:20).

The Resurrection of Christ is not merely the memory of a past event. On Easter night, in the sacrament of Baptism, resurrection, the victory over death, is truly achieved.

Confession—"It is this that we need"

The confession of one's own sin can seem to be something heavy for the person, because it humbles his pride and confronts him with his poverty. It is this that we need: we suffer exactly for this reason: we shut ourselves up in our delirium of guiltlessness and for this reason we are closed to others and to any comparison with them. In psychotherapeutic treatments a person is made to bear the burden of profound and often dangerous revelations of his inner self. In the Sacrament of Penance, the simple confession of one's guilt is presented with confidence in God's merciful goodness. It is important to do this without falling into scruples, with the spirit of trust proper to the children of God. In this way confession can become an experience of deliverance, in which the weight of the past is removed from us and we can feel rejuvenated by the merit of the grace of God who each time gives back the youthfulness of the heart.

"The Eucharist creates charity."

The Eucharist builds the Church, it builds this great network of communion that is the Body of Christ and thereby creates charity.

"Into the new Jerusalem"

Thus the Eucharist is a process of transformations, drawing on God's power to transform hatred and violence, on his power to transform the world. We must therefore pray that the Lord will help us to celebrate and to live the Eucharist in this way. We pray that he transform us, and together with us the world, into the new Jerusalem.

The Eucharist—"The heart of Christian life"

The Eucharist, the heart of Christian life and the source of the evangelizing mission of the Church, cannot but be the permanent center and the source of the petrine service entrusted to me.

"The Eucharist makes the Risen Christ constantly present, Christ who continues to give himself to us, calling us to participate in the banquet of his Body and his Blood. From this full communion with him comes every other element of the life of the Church, in the first place the communion among the faithful, the commitment to proclaim and give witness to the Gospel, the ardor of charity towards all, especially toward the poor and the smallest."

The Eucharist—"To live in view of the resurrection"

The purpose of the Eucharist is the transformation of those who receive it in authentic communion. And so the end is unity, that peace which we, as separate individuals who live beside one another or in conflict with one another, become with Christ and in him, as one organism of self-giving, to live in view of the resurrection and the new world. It is truly the one, identical Lord, whom we receive in the Eucharist, or better, the Lord who receives us and assumes us into himself. St. Augustine expressed this in a short passage which he perceived as a sort of vision: eat the bread of the strong; you will not transform me into yourself, but I will transform you into me. In other words, when we consume bodily nourishment, it is assimilated by the body, becoming itself a part of ourselves. But this bread is of another type. It is greater and higher than we are. It is not we who assimilate it, but it assimilates us to itself, so that we become in a certain way "conformed to Christ," as Paul says, members of his body, one in him.

Two great saints

The great social saints were in reality always also the great Eucharistic saints. I would like only to mention two examples chosen entirely at random. First of all, the beloved figure of St. Martin de Porres, who was born in 1569 in Lima, Peru, the son of an Afro-American mother and a Spanish nobleman. Martin lived from the adoration of the Lord present in the Eucharist, passing entire nights in prayer before the crucifix, while during the day he tirelessly cared for the sick and assisted the socially outcast and despised, with whom he, as a mulatto, identified because of his origins. The encounter with the Lord, who gives himself to us from the cross, makes all of us members of the one body by means of the one bread, which when responded to fully moves us to serve the suffering, to care for the weak and the forgotten.

In our time, the image of Mother Teresa of Calcutta is before the eyes of all. Wherever she opened the houses of her sisters to the service of the dying and outcast, the first thing she asked for was a place for the tabernacle, because she knew that only beginning from there could come the strength for such service.

The Celebration of the Christian Mystery

"The Celebration of the Christian Mystery." This means that the sacraments are envisaged entirely in terms of salvation history, based upon the Paschal mystery—the Paschal center of the life and work of Christ—as a representation of the Paschal mystery, in which we are included. This also means that the sacraments are understood entirely as liturgy, in terms of the concrete liturgical celebration. In this the Catechism has accomplished an important step beyond the traditional neo-scholastic teaching on the sacraments. Already medieval theology to a large extent had separated the theological consideration of the sacraments from their liturgical realization and, proceeding from this, treated the categories of institution, sign, efficacy, minister, and recipient, such that only what referred to the sign kept a connection with the liturgical celebration. Certainly, the sign was not considered so much in the living and concrete liturgical form, as it was analyzed according to the philosophical categories of matter and form. Increasingly, liturgy and theology were ever more separated from one another; dogmatics did not interpret the liturgy, rather its abstract theological content, so that the liturgy appeared almost to be a collection of ceremonies, which clothed the essential—the matter and the form—and for this reason could also be replaceable. In its turn, the "liturgical science" (to the extent to which one can call this a science) became a teaching of the liturgical norms in force and thus came closer to becoming a sort of juridical positivism. The liturgical movement of the 1920's tried to overcome this dangerous separation and sought to understand the nature of the sacraments based upon their liturgical form; to understand the liturgy not simply as a more or less casual collection of ceremonies, but as the development of what came from within the sacrament to have its consistent expression in the liturgical celebration.

Celebrating the Eucharist

I am convinced that the ecclesial crisis in which we find ourselves today depends in great part upon the collapse of the liturgy, which at times is actually being conceived *etsi Deus non daretur:* as though in the liturgy it did not matter anymore whether God exists and whether He speaks to us and listens to us. But if in the liturgy the communion of faith no longer appears, nor the universal unity of the Church and of her history, nor the mystery of the living Christ, where is it that the Church still appears in her spiritual strength? . . .

Matrimony—"A kind of Death"

Love is always a kind of death. We die again and again in marriage, in the family, and in all our dealings with fellow men. The power of selfishness can be explained in the light of this experience. It is a flight—an all too understandable flight—from the mystery of death that is love. At the same time, however, it is only this death that is love which is really fruitful.

Holy Orders

The priestly ministry was born in the Cenacle, together with the Eucharist, as my venerated predecessor John Paul II underlined so many times. "The priestly life must have in a special way a 'Eucharistic form'," he wrote in his last Letter for Holy Thursday. The devout daily celebration of Holy Mass, the center of the life and mission of every priest, contributes to this end.

TODAY'S WORLD

Pope Benedict recognizes that leading a moral life may appear difficult and may require sacrifice. But, in the end, he argues, it is the easiest and most joyful way to live a human life. He believes that certain actions and behaviors can be said to be wrong, and that they lead human beings into misery and toward death. But he also points out the dangers of a false piety that merely follows the rules out of fear or without joy and conviction, like the brother of the Prodigal Son. Such morality can lead a person to refuse to partake of the banquet, and be just as damaging as actual immorality.

In the ordinary course of human life, there is no greater happiness for human beings than the happiness of being in a family. Inside a family, the barriers of suspicions and mistrust that are so common in our world are down. Beginning with the love between a husband and a wife, a family is a series of interlocking relationships of trust and love. Both mothers and fathers take pleasure in loving their children and providing them with a safe and happy home. And the children's experience of this love provides the foundation for all the loving relationships of their lives. This natural joy can be marred by sin and the family can be fractured and broken. But precisely because it is fragile, it is precious. For Pope Benedict, the family is a treasure which society ought to support and sustain by all possible means. He believes that one of the chief goals of the Church and the Church's ministers is to provide a framework within which young people may be nurtured and guided so that they can enter marriage with a deep understanding of the meaning of their love. The Church's teaching about sexual morality is directed to this end, so that the natural joy of family life may be deep and enduring.

The Pope grieves for all of the pain and horror that have occurred in human history through the passions and sins of men, including the Nazi persecution of the Jews and other genocides and persecutions throughout history. But he also insists that history is not all tragedy. He celebrates the struggles to build livable cities and nations, to cultivate and care for the earth, to explore through science the wonders of nature, to create cultures and civilizations where human beings can live with dignity. In his reflections on human history, the Pope sees a pattern in which God's providence seems to be drawing the world toward an as yet unrevealed destination.

In Christian belief, history is not eternal but will have an end, and this end is not to be feared because it is the threshold of an eternal reality toward which human history is ordered.

Politics is that area of human experience which seems to exercise the greatest influence over our daily lives: how much freedom we have, how much prosperity, how much poverty, etc. Benedict believes that certain systems of government can be inimical to human dignity and happiness. He has particularly opposed fanaticism and ideologies which run roughshod over individual persons for the sake of a "cause." For example, he has criticized the Marxist notion of "class conflict," which lumps people by class without regard to individuality. For him, it is necessary always to defend certain fundamental standards of human dignity and life regardless of the views of the majority.

Any attempt to express human hopes and fears, joys and sorrows, love of beauty, in the various mediums of art—music, painting, sculpture, drama, poetry, etc.—is noble and praiseworthy, according to Pope Benedict. These creations of human ingenuity form a tissue of interpretation of experience which contributes to the understanding and enjoyment of our world. Still, art too may fall into periods of decadence, as can entire cultures. For Benedict, the Christian faith has historically been able to provide certain deep insights and values which have contributed to reaching the heights of artistic excellence and spiritual power.

Regarding modernity, Benedict considers the relatively short span of two centuries since the European enlightenment as undermining traditional patterns of family and community life. This characteristic of our highly urbanized and atomized societies has brought about a deep sense of "alienation" in modern society; a "de-sacralization" which has progressed to the point where religious believers have difficulty finding social acceptance. This de facto "totalitarianism of the secular" is one of the great evils of modernity, the Pope believes. True human freedom and true human happiness require a connection with the transcendent. In this sense, he is a profound critic of the spiritual malaise which characterizes modernity.

With respect to ecumenism and other religions, Benedict

has made it very clear that he wishes relations between all Christians to be closer and stronger. He also stressed that he wishes to be in a posture of openness to thoughtful dialogue with believers of other faiths.

The last 15 years have seen the end of the Soviet Union and the unification of Europe. Like the reality of various religious faiths, it is also inescapable that today's world is plagued by the continuation of war, particularly those in the Middle East and the Balkans. Pope Benedict, like his namesake Benedict XV, wishes to persuade governments to avoid war and build a just peace. He has reflected on these questions often in his writings.

Also looming now over the future of mankind are a number of other grave challenges for the future, such as new biotechnological industries and the very low birthrate in much of the industrialized world, particularly in Europe. Pope Benedict has proposed specific solutions to many of these challenges and encourages thoughtful analyses of them all.

⚜ XI ⚜

MORALITY

"A pact with death"

That the loss of the reference to the wise creative plan of God is the profound root of the bewilderment of contemporary man and of his fear in the face of freedom can be suggested to us by a meditation on the second chapter of the book of Wisdom. There the foolish conclusions of the "impious" (that is, those who do not acknowledge that life has any meaning) are spoken of. The "impious" say: "We are born by chance and after we shall be as if we had never been born" (2:2). Scandalized by the fragility of life and by the prospect of death in which it seems to conclude, these "impious" deny any wise and good design and thus resolve to dedicate themselves to the heedless enjoyment of the moment. But inevitably the negation of a meaning and of a responsibility leads to abuses, to injustice toward the weak, to persecution of whomever is just and bears witness to a meaning. In reality, the impious have made a pact with death, they "invoke death upon themselves with gestures and words, considering death a friend, and they consume themselves for her" (1:16). A freedom, disconnected from a responsible reference to the wise plan of God and left to itself in a world of chance, is secretly undermined by a pact with death, which ends up by destroying it.

"Largely shattered"

The moral question has become more clearly than ever before the question of mankind's survival. In the homogenous, technical civilization which now encompasses the entire world, the old moral certainties that up to now have sustained the great individual cultures have been largely shattered. The technical view of the world is value-free. It asks not "Ought we?" but "Can we?" Indeed, to many the question of the "ought" appears outdated, irreconcilable with the emancipation of man from all constraints. What one can do, one should do, many think today.

Permissivism to prevail?

In a world like the West, where money and wealth are the measures of all things, and where the model of the free market imposes its implacable laws on every aspect of life, authentic Catholic ethics now appears to many like an alien body from times long past . . . Economic liberalism creates its exact counterpart, *permissivism,* on the moral plane.

"He alone is good."

The rich young man asked the Lord the question: "What good must I do to have eternal life?" (Matthew 19:16) This conversation does not belong to the past. We are all caught up in it. We pose the question perhaps in another form, but we want to know what we should do to attain a fulfilled life . . . In this penetrating listening to the words of Christ, it emerges that the search for the good is inseparably connected to the turn toward God. He alone is good without limitation. The good *par excellence* in a person. Jesus asks us to follow him, and to imitate him along the path of love, a love which gives itself completely to the brethren out of love for God.

⚜ XII ⚜

MARRIAGE AND FAMILY LIFE

Monogamous marriage is a basic form of order of the relations between men and women and at the same time a cell of national community and education formed from the biblical faith. Marriage gave Europe, both in the East and in the West, a special feature and a particular humanity . . . Europe would no longer be Europe if this basic cell of its social structure would diminish or substantially change. We all know how endangered marriage and family is nowadays—

due to the hollowing out of indissolvability through ever easier forms of divorce ... We are before the dissolution of the human image whose consequences will only be extremely grave.

❧ XIII ❧

SOCIAL JUSTICE

Peace

Peace can never last on earth if God becomes meaningless to people. Christian efforts for peace must therefore concentrate, among other things, on making clear the hierarchy of values and the hierarchy of evils. Working for peace must mean teaching people to recognize what makes for peace.

"In this passing world"

To be workers of true justice, we must be workers who are being made just by contact with him who is justice itself: Jesus of Nazareth. The place of this encounter is the Church, nowhere more powerfully present than in her sacraments and liturgy.

In the mystery of Good Friday, God is judged by man and condemned by human justice. In the Easter Vigil, the light of God's justice banishes the darkness of sin and death; the stone at the tomb ... is pushed away forever, and human life is given a future which, in going beyond the categories of this world, reveals the true meaning and the true value of earthly realities.

We who have been baptized, as children of a world

which is still to come, in the liturgy of the Easter Vigil, catch a glimpse of that world and breathe the atmosphere of that world, where God's justice will dwell forever. Then, renewed and transformed by the Mysteries we celebrate, we can walk in this world justly, living—as the Preface for Lent says so beautifully—"in this passing world with our heart set on the world that will never end."

"A single great cry of sorrow"

It is undeniable that the liberal model of the market economy, especially as moderated and corrected under the influence of Christian social ideas, has in some parts of the world led to great successes. All the sadder are the results, especially in places like Africa, where clashing power blocs and economic interests have been at work. Behind the apparent beneficial models of development there has all too often been hidden the desire to expand the reach of particular powers and ideologies in order to dominate markets. In this situation, ancient social structures and spiritual and moral forces have been destroyed, with consequences that echo in our ears like a single great cry of sorrow. One thing is clear: without God things cannot go well. And because only in Christ has God shown us his face, spoken his name, entered into communion with us; without Christ there is no ultimate hope.

Justice

Classical theology, as we know, understands the virtue of justice as composed of two elements which for Christians cannot be separated; justice is the firm will to render to God what is owed to God, and to our neighbor what is owed to him; indeed, justice toward God is what we call the "virtue of religion"; justice toward other human beings is the fundamental attitude that respects the other as a person created by God.

God condemned

In the mystery of Good Friday, God is judged by man and condemned by human justice.

Transforming the world

Christ's love is love for the poor and the suffering. We know well that our Popes were strongly committed to fighting against injustice and for the rights of the oppressed and the weak. Christ's love is not something individualistic, solely spiritual: it concerns the flesh, it concerns the world, and it must transform the world.

Adoration

There is a phrase of the German Jesuit, Alfred Delp, executed by the Nazis: "Bread is important, freedom is more important, but the thing most important of all is adoration." Where this order of goods is not respected, but overturned, and justice no longer derived, the encounter with the man who suffers no longer takes place, but even the area of material goods is thrown into turmoil and destroyed. Where God is seen as a secondary power, that one can temporarily or completely set aside because of more important things, then precisely those presumably more important things also fail.

Not only the negative outcome of the Marxist experiment shows this. The development assistance given by the West based on purely technical-material principles, which not only have left God aside, but have distanced men from God in the arrogance of their presumption, have principally done great harm to the third world, the Third World in the contemporary sense. It has left aside the existing religious, moral, and social structures and has introduced its technician-like mentality into the void. It believed it could transform the stones into bread, but it has given stones instead of bread. We must recognize anew the primacy of God and of his Word.

"We must not sleep again"

Justice is no longer to be circumscribed by the boundaries of one country. North and south, rich nations and poor, form one world in which the fate of one group is not to be separated from that of another ... Only when we keep in mind the justice of the whole world can we rightfully discern what justice means for us here and now. Only when we find, in the self-determination of the Christian Faith and its moral force, the initiative for a Christian justice for the whole world, can there be an end to the destructive message of violence, which is overweening wherever egoism is stronger than right. As Christians, we must not sleep again in a time of crisis, as happened to some extent in the nineteenth century.

"Violence solves no problems"

... Solidarity includes justice as its central demand. We are solidaristic only when we give to others what is rightfully theirs by reason of their creatureliness, their humanity. For us, therefore, the foundation of all economic and social relationship is not confrontation but charity and cooperation. Confrontation is destruction. Violence solves no problems ... It follows, then, that the great social achievements, the gradual construction of a system of social justice, do not owe their existence to the program of Karl Marx, whose disciples wanted, not reform, but a progressive deterioration that would pave the way for their paradise. What are we to conclude from all this? To the concept of a class struggle and its inhumane utopias we are to oppose the fundamental principle of solidarity and justice. The decision as to what is right or not right is not to be made lightly. Respect for what is right is the basis of every human community. Without it, there is, in the long run, no respect for humanity itself and no preservation of human dignity.

"Lofty words"

How often are the symbols of power, borne by the great ones of this world, an affront to truth, to justice, and to the dignity of man! How many times are their pomp and their lofty words nothing but grandiose lies, a parody of their solemn obligation to serve the common good!

"Our true greatness"

Let us strip away our sense of self-sufficiency, our false illusions of independence, and learn from him, the One who humbled himself, to discover our true greatness by bending low before God and before our downtrodden brothers and sisters.

⚜ XIV ⚜

HUMAN HISTORY

"Europe seems to have become empty."

A strange unhappiness about the future exists in Europe. This is most visible on the aspect that children are viewed as a threat of the present; they are no longer seen as a hope, but moreover a border of the present. In the hour of its greatest success, Europe seems to have become empty inside, paralyzed by a life-threatening crisis to its health . . .

"Blessed are the meek."

Power has become the sign of our times. Meekness, gentleness are not greatly appreciated. Generally speaking, it is almost impossible to use the words meekness or gentleness even among Christians without arousing misgivings and rejection. Undoubtedly a portion of the guilt here is borne by the many caricatures of meekness that fail to recognize the courage of the meekness and the courage of the truth that have their source in love. And yet we cannot overcome the climate of power that threatens all of us unless we resolutely oppose it to a culture of humaneness, a culture of meekness.

"A sign is given."

How often we find ourselves fearing that there is, after all, no meaning in the chaotic flurry of this world . . . There is a general feeling that the powers of darkness are on the increase, that the good is powerless . . . Will the good continue to have meaning and power in the world? In the stable at Bethlehem a sign is given that enables us to answer with a joyous Yes! For the Child, God's only-begotten Son, is set as a sign and a surety that in the end God will have the last word in world history and that he is truth and love.

"The poisoning of man"

Goethe once termed struggle between belief and unbelief the great theme of world history, picking up a theme of Augustine's philosophy of history. Augustine, himself, of course, expressed this differently: he sees in world history the struggle between two kinds of love: love for self, which goes as far as despising God, and love for God, which goes as far as despising oneself. Today, we can perhaps formulate this in still another way: history is marked by the confrontation between love and the inability to love, that devastation of the soul that comes when the only values man is able to recognize at all as values are quantifiable values. The capacity to love, that is, the capacity to wait in patience for what is not under one's own control and to let oneself receive this as a gift, is suffocated by the speedy fulfillments in which I am dependent on no one, but in which I am never obliged to emerge from my own self, and thus never find the path into my own self. This destruction of the capacity to love gives birth to lethal boredom. It is the poisoning of man.

XV

POLITICS AND PEACE

"The foundation of freedom"

The aim of the Church's political stand must be to maintain the balance of a dual system as the foundation of freedom. Hence the Church must make claims and demands on public law, and cannot simply retreat into the private sphere. Hence it must also take care on the other hand that Church and State remain separated and that belonging to the Church clearly retains its voluntary character.

Democratic socialism

Democratic socialism has been able to add itself as a healthy counterbalance to the radical liberal positions of both existing models (the secular and the State-Church model). It enriched and corrected them. It proved itself even when the confessions took over: in England, it was the party of the Catholics which felt at home neither in the Protestant-Conservative nor in the liberal camp. Also in Wilhelmine Germany, the Catholic center could continue to feel closer to Democratic Socialism than to the Conservative powers. In many aspects, Democratic Socialism stands and stood close to Catholic social teachings. In any case, it contributed a substantial amount to the education of social conscience.

On law and peace

International law has developed in our century into a total banning of war and violence—admittedly, a great achievement. But very quickly an expert on international law expressed his fear that precisely this step would be the prelude to an age of world wars. Have not subsequent events proved him right? Major wars have, thank God, ceased to exist (for the time being, at least). But are we not experiencing, at the same time, the increasing destruction of the peaceful order within nations? Do we not witness the disintegration of the zone of peace created by the common domestic laws of nations? Where domestic peace disintegrates, where a violence based on ideologies comes to be taken for granted or even as a virtue for noble souls, the way to great violence stands open. Thus we see again how crucial it is to build dams to prevent the disintegration of law within nations and to protect, with all possible determination, the moral value of the Christian tradition.

Freedom

Freedom, in order to be true, human freedom, freedom in truth, needs communion. An isolated freedom, a freedom only for the "I," would be a lie, and would destroy human communion. In order to be true, and therefore in order to be efficient, freedom needs communion, and not just any kind of communion, but ultimately communion with truth itself, with love itself, with Christ, with the Trinitarian God. Thus is built community that creates freedom and gives joy.

Poverty

A first group of his (Don Luigi Giussani's) followers went to Brazil and found itself face to face with extreme poverty, with extreme misery. What can be done? How can we respond? And there was a great temptation to say, "For the moment we have to set Christ aside, set God aside, because there are more pressing needs, we have first to change the structure, the external things, first we must improve the earth, then we can find heaven again." It was the great temptation of that moment to transform Christianity into a moralism and moralism into politics, to substitute believing with doing. Because what does faith imply? We can say, "In this moment we have to do something." And all the same, in this way, by substituting faith with moralism, believing with doing, we fall into particularisms, we lose most of all the criteria and the orientations, and in the end we don't build, but divide.

Monsignor Giussani, with his fearless and unfailing faith, knew that, even in this situation, Christ, the encounter with Him, remains central, because whoever does not give God, gives too little, and whoever does not give God, whoever does not make people find God in the Fact of Christ, does not build, but destroys, because he gets human activity lost in ideological and false dogmatisms.

Fr. Giussani kept the centrality of Christ and, exactly in this way, with social works, with necessary service, he helped mankind in this difficult world, where the responsibility of Christians for the poor in the world is enormous and urgent.

Sacrifice

It is clear that we must develop our economy in a way that it no longer operates only to further the interests of a certain country or group of countries, but for the welfare of the world. This is difficult and is never fully realized. It requires that we make sacrifices. But if a spirit of solidarity is truly nourished, faith is born; then this could become possible, even if always in an imperfect way.

⚜ XVI ⚜

CULTURE AND THE ARTS

"It is always a gift"

Art cannot be "produced," as one contracts out and produces technical equipment. It is always a gift. Inspiration is not something one can choose for oneself. It has to be received, otherwise it is not there. One cannot bring about a renewal of art in faith by money or through commissions. Before all things it requires the gift of a new kind of seeing. And so it would be worth our while to regain a faith that sees. Wherever that exists, art finds its proper expressions.

The arrow that strikes the heart

The arrow of the beautiful can guide the mind to the truth . . . The encounter with the beautiful can become the wound of the arrow that strikes the heart and in this way opens our eyes, so that later, from this experience, we take the criteria for judgment and can correctly evaluate the arguments.

Beauty of the icon: fasting of sight

An icon does not simply reproduce what can be perceived by the senses, but rather it presupposes, as he says, "a fasting of sight." Inner perception must free itself from the impression of the merely sensible, and in prayer and ascetical effort acquire a new and deeper capacity to see, to perform the passage from what is merely external to the profundity of reality, in such a way that the artist can see what the senses as such do not see, and what actually appears in what can be perceived: the splendor of the glory of God, the "glory of God shining on the face of Christ" (II Cor 4,6). To admire the icons and the great masterpieces of Christian art in general leads us on an inner way, a way of overcoming ourselves; thus in this purification of vision that is a purification of the heart, it reveals the beautiful to us, or at least a ray of it. In this way we are brought into contact with the power of the truth.

Christian art

So it is that Christian art today is caught between two fires (as perhaps it always has been): it must oppose the cult of the ugly, which says that everything beautiful is a deception and only the representation of what is crude, low, and vulgar is the truth, the true illumination of knowledge. Or it has to counter the deceptive beauty that makes the human being seem diminished instead of making him great, and for this reason is false.

Beethoven

Beethoven's Ninth Symphony echoes the inner strife of the great maestro in the midst of the darkness of life, his passage, as it were, through dark nights in which none of the promised stars seemed any longer to shine in the heavens. But in the end, the clouds lift. The great drama of human existence that unfolds in the music is transformed into a hymn of joy for which Beethoven borrowed the words of Schiller, whose true greatness blossomed only through his music.

Handel

We are indebted to Georg Friedrich Handel for another incomparable hymn of joy: the great *Alleluia*, which is the crowning moment of his *Messiah*. In it he set to music promise and fulfillment, the prophecy of the Redeemer who was to come and the historical events of the life of Jesus to which it corresponds. The *Alleluia* is the song of praise of the redeemed who, through Christ's Resurrection, can still rejoice, even amid the sufferings of this world. This great musical tradition—as we will experience in these hours— has lived on through all the vicissitudes of history, and is a ray of light in which the star of faith, the presence of Jesus Christ, continues to shine.

Beethoven, Bach, Schiller

Compared with the intact presence of the faith that transpires in Handel's hymn to joy and which emerges in a very different way, that is, as a tranquil inner peace and the grace of reconciliation, in Bach's Christmas Oratorio or at the end of his Passions, the illuminating "Ode" by Schiller, so impressively set to music by Beethoven, is characterized by the humanism of that time, which places man at the center and—where there is a reference to God—prefers the language of myth.

Nevertheless, we should not forget that Beethoven is also the composer of the *Missa Solemnis*. The good Father, of which the "Ode" speaks, is not so much a supposition, as Schiller's text might suggest, but rather, an ultimate certainty. Beethoven also knew that we can entrust ourselves to the Father because in the Son he made himself close to us. And thus, we can calmly see the divine spark, of whose joy the "Ode" speaks, as that spark of God which is communicated to us through the music and reassures us: yes, the good Father truly exists and is not utterly remote, far beyond the firmament, but thanks to the Son is here in our midst.

XVII

MODERNITY

"A century of suffering"

We can recognize the last century as a century of martyrs, a century of suffering and persecution for the Church, a century of world wars and the many local wars which filled the last fifty years and have inflicted unprecedented forms of cruelty ... To understand the signs of the times means to accept the urgency of penance, of conversion, of faith. This is the correct response to this moment of history, characterized by the grave perils outlined in the images that follow.

An archaic relic?

Religion today is considered an archaic relic to be left alone because, finally, it is thought to have nothing to do with the true greatness of progress. What religions say and do appears totally irrelevant; they are not even a part of the world of rationality, their contents ultimately count for nothing.

"Divine protection is not commandeered."

Granted, we speak all the more frequently about security and about how we can protect ourselves against the negative aspects of modern life. The flight of humanity from its own work is on the increase, and we come to recognize the inadequacy of our protective devices—however sophisticated they may be—only when new refinements reveal that they have already been superseded. It would, of course, be foolish and unrealistic on our part to place our trust in guardian angels rather than in technology; the divine protection is not so easily commandeered and is not intended to be thrown into bold relief. Speaking of angels means being convinced that the world is everywhere filled with the divine presence of God and that his presence is bestowed on each and every one of us as a power that summons and protects us.

⚜ XVIII ⚜

ECUMENISM AND OTHER RELIGIONS

Building peace

The world in which we live is often marked by conflicts, violence, and war, but it earnestly longs for peace, peace which is above all a gift from God, peace for which we must pray without ceasing. Yet peace is also a duty to which all peoples must be committed, especially those who profess to belong to religious traditions. Our efforts to come together and foster dialogue are a valuable contribution to building peace on solid foundations. Pope John Paul II, my venerable predecessor, wrote at the start of the new Millennium that "the name of the one God must become increasingly what it is: a name of peace and a summons to peace" (*Novo Millennio Ineunte*, 55). It is therefore imperative to engage in authentic and sincere dialogue, built on respect for the dignity of every human person, created, as we Christians firmly believe, in the image and likeness of God (cf. Gen 1:26-27).

Islam and the Koran

It is true on one hand that Christianity has always considered itself to be the true religion, that is, open to reason, and on the other that Islam considers itself perfectly reasonable, but the concept of reason is different. Even the concept of God's action is different. For example, the Koran is considered to be a word that comes immediately, as such, directly from God, without human mediation. While for us, the Sacred Scripture evolved out of God's history with his people, with the mediation of man's response to God, involving man in God's action. This is only an example of how, while having many elements in common, there is a profound difference in the foundations of the two realities. Any dialogue must certainly appeal to reason and try to see how reason can help us in this dialogue. A great deal of patience is needed so that, in profound allegiance to the Revelation and the openness that this generates, we can leave it to the Lord to mark out the path for this dialogue.

"Islam has had moments of great splendor."

It is true that the Muslim world is not totally mistaken when it reproaches the West of Christian tradition for moral decadence and the manipulation of human life . . . Islam has also had moments of great splendor and decadence in the course of its history.

Protestantism

Protestantism originated at the beginning of the modern age and is consequently much more closely allied than Catholicism to the inner forces that generated the modern age. The present form of Protestantism is due in large measure to its encounter with the great philosophical movements of the nineteenth century. It is its destiny and its danger that it is wide open to modern thought. Consequently, it is precisely among those Catholic theologians who are no longer satisfied with traditional theology that the conviction is to be found that the right ways to unite faith and modernity have already been laid in Protestantism.

Today's average Christian assumes on the basis of this principle that faith is a product of the individual point of view, of intellectual endeavor, and of the work of specialists, and such a point of view seems to him more modern and more self-evident than the Catholic positions. For many today it is hardly comprehensible that a mysterious divine reality lies behind the human reality. But, as we know, that is the Catholic understanding of Church.

Non-Christians

Inevitably, Christians began asking whether they had the right simply to destroy the world of the other religions, or whether it was not possible, or even imperative, to understand the other religions from within and integrate their inheritance into Christianity. In this way, ecumenism eventually expanded into inter-religious dialogue ... in order to understand religion, it is necessary to experience it from within, indeed, that only such experience, which is inevitably particular and tied to a definite historical starting-point, can lead the way to mutual understanding and thus to a deepening and purification of religion.

Seeking religious unity

Thus, in full awareness and at the beginning of his ministry in the Church of Rome that Peter bathed with his blood, the current Successor assumes as his primary commitment that of working tirelessly towards the reconstitution of the full and visible unity of all Christ's followers. This is his ambition, this is his compelling duty. He is aware that to do so, expressions of good feelings are not enough. Concrete gestures are required to penetrate souls and move consciences, encouraging everyone to that interior conversion which is the basis for all progress on the road of ecumenism.

Theological dialogue is necessary. A profound examination of the historical reasons behind past choices is also indispensable. But even more urgent is that "purification of memory," which was so often evoked by John Paul II, and which alone can dispose souls to welcome the full truth of Christ. It is before him, supreme Judge of all living things, that each of us must stand, in the awareness that one day we must explain to Him what we did and what we did not do for the great good that is the full and visible unity of all His disciples.

The current Successor of Peter feels himself to be personally implicated in this question and is disposed to do all in his power to promote the fundamental cause of ecumenism. In the wake of his predecessors, he is fully determined to cultivate any initiative that may seem appropriate to promote contact and agreement with representatives from the various Churches and ecclesial communities. Indeed, on this occasion too, he sends them his most cordial greetings in Christ, the one Lord of all.

"With simplicity and affection"

I address myself to everyone, even to those who follow other religions or who are simply seeking an answer to the fundamental questions of life and have not yet found it. I address everyone with simplicity and affection, to assure them that the Church wants to continue to build an open and sincere dialogue with them, in a search for the true good of mankind and of society.

⚜ XIX ⚜

BIOETHICS

"Unimaginable consequences"

Biological manipulation is striving to uncouple man from nature . . . At the end of this march to shatter fundamental, natural linkages (and not, as is said, only those that are cultural), there are unimaginable consequences which, however, derive from the very logic that lies at the base of a venture of this kind.

"Not justifiable"

Whether we think of cloning or the cultivation of human fetuses for the purpose of scientific research, organ transplants, or the entire area of genetic manipulation, the silent devastation of human dignity which is threatening no one can overlook. The "good purposes" are always put forward to justify something which is not justifiable. To this adds the growing number in human trafficking, new forms of slavery, the commerce of human organs for the purpose of transplantation.

"The world reaches for the stones."

When the Church's work for justice touches on issues and problems which the world no longer sees as bound up with human dignity, like protecting the right to life of every human being from conception to natural death, or when the Church confesses that justice also includes our responsibilities toward God himself, then the world not infrequently reaches for the stones mentioned in our Gospel today.

As Christians we must constantly be reminded that the call of justice is not something which can be reduced to the categories of this world.

Reason

Thomas Aquinas writes that the natural law "is nothing other than the light of understanding infused in us by God." The natural law is a law of reason. To have reason is the nature of men. When it is said that our nature is the measure of freedom, reason is not then eliminated; rather, full justice is accorded it. With such statements, in order to avoid falling into error, we must recall what is typical of human reason, that it is not absolute like God's reason. It belongs to a created being, to be sure, to a creature in whom body and soul are inseparable. Finally, it belongs to a being who stands in historical alienation, which can impair the capacity of reason to see.

❧ XX ❧

CHALLENGES FOR THE FUTURE

The future of the Church...will be a spiritualized Church that does not rely on a political mandate and that curries favor with the right as little as with the left. It will be a difficult time for the Church. For the process of crystallization and clarification will cost her much valuable energy. It will make her poor, will make her a Church of the meek. The process will be all the harder because it will be just as necessary to root out sectarian narrow-mindedness as boastful self-will. The way will be long and wearisome, just as was the way that led from the false progressivism on the eve of the French Revolution...But after the purification of these uprootings a great strength will emanate from a spiritualized and simplified Church...It seems certain to me that very hard times await the Church. Her own crisis has as yet hardly begun.

THE CHRISTIAN PILGRIM

I f God is good, why is there evil and suffering in the world? This has always been a mystery for believers. In the end, Pope Benedict argues, it is human freedom which seems to be the most priceless value in the providence of God. For, through freedom there comes true love. But Adam's freedom was the source of the suffering, sin and death that entered the world. It is in this dynamic of sin and freedom and love that the Pope seeks the hidden key to the meaning of both freedom and suffering.

Some philosophers argue that if human beings knew all the consequences of their actions, for good and for ill, they would never do evil, never commit a sin. There is often truth in this notion of sin as a result of ignorance, Pope Benedict believes. But it is not the complete truth. Human beings are capable of choosing evil even when they know it is evil and will have evil consequences. The Pope sees the only response to the problem of humans persisting in deliberate evil is cooperation with God's grace and radical conversion to Christ.

All partings, it is said, are little deaths. But there is one parting, death, after which there can be no reunion in this world. However, for Benedict XVI, as for all Christians, death does not have the final word. For him, there is another meeting after our mortal flesh breathes its last, when the soul enters the world of eternity. It is a meeting with Christ. Where does this meeting take place? In the place prepared by God and promised by Jesus after his resurrection. Plants are nourished by drawing water and minerals from the soil and the energy of the sun from the air. Trees planted by rivers and in full sunlight grow vigorously. Animals are nourished by eating plants or other animals or both. Men and women, as persons, nourish their physical bodies on water and plants and meat and fish. But "man does not live by bread alone." Human beings live by being nourished on another level, by what may be called "spiritual food." Without this nourishment, a person's spiritual life can shrivel and eventually die. With this nourishment, a person's spirit can flourish. Prayer connects the soul and the transcendent God. Through prayer, the trials, struggles, and joys of this world can be shared, burdens lightened, and inner joys experienced. Above all, friendship with Christ and the saints, and conversations with God, deepen the capacity of the human heart to face all troubles with hope.

Faith, according to scripture, is the "evidence of things not seen." Since involving "things unseen," Faith cannot be proved by scientific experiment, but this does not mean that faith is irrational. Faith transcends human reason, but it does not contradict it. For the Pope, faith is that anchor which believers cast out toward God that, in the very act of being cast, fixes itself solidly in an invisible seabed. Faith is an act both of the intellect and of the will, involving the whole personality. When a person believes, he is different from when he doubts. Faith changes a person, providing a structure and framework for the spirit.

Without hope we are in the dark, or more precisely, despair. In the Christian tradition, some have argued that the only unforgivable sin is despair. In fact, Jesus named the unforgivable sin as "the sin against the Holy Spirit." A person in despair may contemplate taking his own life because suicide is an act of hopelessness. Hope, therefore, is a spiritual grace which counters the tendency toward despair. It is the function of all Christian doctrines and sacraments to lead toward hope and away from despair. The great hope of Christians is God and his love.

Without love, human life has no savor, no joy. Love is a force of attraction which draws the person toward the beloved. To love is to be drawn ultimately toward what is good and beautiful and true. But love can be blind, mistaken, and false. The search for love that is true can require great discernment and sacrifice. Pope Benedict's meditations on love include some of his most beautiful and moving passages.

Holiness, a great mystery, by its very nature participates in the divine because, by definition, God alone is holy. Since no man can know God, holiness itself in some way transcends our human capacity to know. And yet, all human societies at all times have had a concept of what we call "holiness." There is a universal human sense of that "numinous reality" (to use the expression of Rudolf Otto, "The Idea of the Holy"), which is different from profane, ordinary reality. A holy place, or a holy person, is always seen as one suffused with a divine energy or quality, "set apart" from ordinary places or persons. Holiness transcends a person's nature and ability. A person becomes holy by allowing and being ready for the hand of God to transform his weakness.

To be a saint, a holy person, is to speak with God as a friend speaks with a friend, to be in a profound relationship with God, becoming a "friend" of God: it is letting the Other work, the Only One who can really make the world both good and happy.

Temporal life has an end. Lived in a series of moments, it is always moving and changing, developing, growing—and decaying. But there is a horizon, an eternity, beyond. The nature of eternal life is inevitably mysterious to all who contemplate it from the perspective of this world.

Jesus says to his apostles that he wishes that their joy should be complete. The Pope has echoed that wish in his writings and in the first words of his pontificate. The aim of the Christian life is not misery and sadness but blessedness and joy. The ultimate aim is the complete gift of self to others and to God and the free return of that gift from others, and from God.

XXI

SUFFERING

Good and evil

Our Lord announces to us that scandals and sinners will be in our community and Church. St. Peter, Prince of the Apostles, was a great sinner, and yet the Lord wanted precisely the sinner Peter as the rock of the Church. Thus he indicated to us not to expect great saints of all the Popes—

we must also expect there to be sinners among them. He announces to us that in the fields of the Church there will be much chaff. This sense should not surprise us if we consider all of Church history. There have been other times at least as difficult as ours with scandals, etc. All we have to do is think of the ninth century, the tenth century, the Renaissance. Therefore, looking at the words of the Lord, at the history of the Church, we can relativize today's scandals. We suffer. We must suffer because they—that is, the scandals—made so many people suffer, and here we are thinking of the victims. Certainly we must do all we can to avoid that these things happen in the future. But on the other hand, we know that the Lord—and this is the essence of the Church—the Lord sat at the table with sinners. This is the definition of the Church: the Lord sits at the table with sinners. Therefore, we cannot be amazed if it is like this. We cannot despair. On the contrary, the Lord said: "I am not here only for the just, but for sinners." We must feel certain that the Lord truly—even today—seeks sinners in order to save us.

Crown of suffering

It is because Jesus is mocked and wears the crown of suffering that he appears as the true King. His scepter is justice (cf. Ps 45:7). The price of justice in this world is suffering: Jesus, the true King, does not reign through violence, but through a love which suffers for us and with us. He takes up the Cross, our cross, the burden of being human, the burden of the world. And so he goes before us and points out to us the way which leads to true life.

No love without suffering

Pain is part of being human. Anyone who really wanted to get rid of suffering would have to get rid of love before anything else, because there can be no love without suffering, because it always demands an element of self-sacrifice, because, given temperamental differences and the drama of situations, it will always bring with it renunciation and pain ... Anyone who has inwardly accepted suffering becomes more mature and more understanding of others, becomes more human.

Sharing suffering

Lord, you opened the eyes and heart of Simon of Cyrene, and you gave him, by his share in your Cross, the grace of faith. Help us to aid our neighbors in need, even when this interferes with our own plans and desires. Help us to realize that it is a grace to be able to share the cross of others and, in this way, know that we are walking with you along the way. Help us to appreciate with joy that, when we share in your suffering and the sufferings of this world, we become servants of salvation and are able to help build up your Body, the Church.

Suffering love

The mercy of Christ is not a cheap grace; it does not presume evil is trivial. Christ carries in his body and on his soul all the weight of evil, and all its destructive force. He burns and transforms evil through suffering, in the fire of his suffering love. The day of vindication and the year of favor meet in the paschal mystery, in Christ's dying and rising. This is the vindication of God: he himself, in the person of the Son, suffers for us. The more we are touched by the mercy of the Lord, the more we draw closer in solidarity with his suffering—and become willing to bear in our flesh "what is lacking in the afflictions of Christ" (Col 1, 24).

✦ XXII ✦

LONELINESS

Unhealable wound

If there existed a loneliness that no word of another could pierce and change, if there existed an isolation so deep that you could no longer reach it, then there would exist that authentic total loneliness and terror that theology calls "hell." From this standpoint, we can define the word exactly: it means a loneliness into which the word of love no longer penetrates and which is, consequently, the true risk of existence. Which of us is not reminded, in this context, of the belief of poets and philosophers of our time that all contacts among men are basically superficial; no one has admittance to the real depth of another. Consequently no one can penetrate the real depth of that other; every encounter, however beautiful it may be, can do no more than anesthetize the unhealable wound of loneliness. In that case, hell, despair—a loneliness as indefinable as it is dreadful—would dwell in the deepest core of our existence. As we know, it was from this standpoint that Sartre developed his anthropology. But even a poet as conciliatory and apparently as serenely unruffled as Hermann Hesse seems to express fundamentally the same thought: "Strange to wander in the mist. Life is loneliness. No one knows the other.

Each is alone!" One thing is, in fact, certain: there is a night whose isolation is penetrated by no voice; there is a door through which we must pass alone: the door of death. All the fear in the world is ultimately the fear of this loneliness. From this, we can understand why the Old Testament has only one word for hell and death: the word *sheol.* In the last analysis, the two are identical. Death is loneliness *par excellence.* But a loneliness that love can no longer penetrate is—hell.

The drying up of hope

According to Thomas Aquinas, the root of despair is to be found in what has been termed *accidie:* for want of a better word we usually translate this as sloth or inertia, by which very much more, and something deeper, is meant than mere idleness, than lacking the inclination to be active. According to Thomas this metaphysical inertia is identical with the "sorrow of the world," the "worldly grief" of which Paul says that it produces death (2 Cor. 7:10). What is it about the mysterious sorrow of this world? Not that long ago this phrase would have seemed obscure if not unreal to us, since it seemed as if the children of this world were much more cheerful than the faithful, who seemed to be prevented from really enjoying life by being tormented by conscientious scruples and probably also glanced enviously across at the unbelievers who seemed to have the entire paradise of earthly delight standing open for them without reservations or anxieties. The great exodus from the Church was thought to be for precisely this reason, that at last people wanted to be free of the burdensome restrictions that meant that in fact not just one tree in the garden but virtually the whole lot seemed to be forbidden . . . It seemed as if only unbelief could set one free to enjoy life. The yoke of Christ did not feel in any way "easy" or "light" for many Christians of the modern age: they experienced it as far too heavy, at least in the form in which they found it presented to them in the Church.

Today, when the promises of unlimited freedom have been made the most of, we are beginning to understand afresh this saying about the "sorrow of the world." The forbidden joys lose their attraction the moment they are no longer forbidden. They had and have to be radicalized, the pitch increasingly raised, and nevertheless seem finally flat and stale because they are all finite while the hunger is for the infinite. Thus today we often see in the faces of young people a remarkable bitterness, a resignation that is far removed from the enthusiasm of youthful ventures into the unknown. The deepest root of this sorrow is the lack of any great hope and the unattainability of any great love: everything one can hope for is known, and all love becomes the disappointment of finiteness in a world whose monstrous surrogates are only a pitiful disguise for profound despair. And in this way the truth becomes ever more tangible that the sorrow of the world leads to death: it is only flirting with death, the ghastly business of playing with power and violence, that is still exciting enough to create an appearance of satisfaction. "If you eat it you must die"—for a long time this has no longer been just a saying from mythology (Gen. 3:3).

After this first attempt at the nature of the "sorrow of the world," otherwise known as metaphysical inertia, or *accidie*, let us have another and closer look at its physiognomy. On this the traditional Christian anthropology says that this kind of sorrow stems from a lack of greatness of soul (*magnanimitas*), from an incapability of believing in the greatness of the human vocation that has been destined for us by God. Man does not trust himself to his own true dimension but wants to be "more realistic." Metaphysical inertia would on this account be identical with that false humility that has become so common today: man does not want to believe that God is concerned about him, knows him, loves him, watches over him, is close to him.

XXIII

SIN

Pride goeth before a fall.

Our pride ... makes us want to be liberated from God and left alone to ourselves ... makes us think that we do not need his eternal love, but can be the masters of our own lives. In this rebellion against truth, in this attempt to be our own god, creator, and judge, we fall headlong and plunge into self-destruction.

How to attain righteousness

Human righteousness can only be attained by abandoning one's own claims and being generous to man and to God. It is the righteousness of "forgive, as we have been forgiven."

Non-negotiable issues

Not all moral issues have the same moral weight as abortion and euthanasia. For example, if a Catholic were to be at odds with the Holy Father on the application of capital punishment or on the decision to wage war, he would not for that reason be considered unworthy to present himself to receive Holy Communion. While the Church exhorts civil authorities to seek peace, not war, and to exercise discretion and mercy in imposing punishment on criminals, it may still be permissible to take up arms to repel an aggressor or to have recourse to capital punishment. There may be a legitimate diversity of opinion even among Catholics about waging war and applying the death penalty, but not however with regard to abortion and euthanasia.

The illusion of beauty?

Today another objection has even greater weight: the message of beauty is thrown into complete doubt by the power of falsehood, seduction, violence, and evil. Can the beautiful be genuine, or, in the end, is it only an illusion? Isn't reality perhaps basically evil? The fear that in the end it is not the arrow of the beautiful that leads us to the truth, but that falsehood, all that is ugly and vulgar, may constitute the true "reality" has at all times caused people anguish. At present this has been expressed in the assertion that after Auschwitz it was no longer possible to write poetry; after Auschwitz it is no longer possible to speak of a God who is good. People wondered: where was God when the gas chambers were operating? This objection, which seemed reasonable enough before Auschwitz when one realized all the atrocities of history, shows that in any case a purely harmonious concept of beauty is not enough. It cannot stand up to the confrontation with the gravity of the questioning about God, truth, and beauty. Apollo, who for Plato's Socrates was "the God" and the guarantor of unruffled beauty as "the truly divine" is absolutely no longer sufficient.

"Stained with grave sins"

It is clear that Christians in past centuries have been stained with grave sins. Slavery and the slave trade remain a dark chapter that show how few Christians were truly Christian and how far many Christians were from the faith and message of the Gospel, from true communion with Jesus Christ. On the other hand, lives full of faith and love, as seen in the humble willingness of so many priests and sisters to sacrifice themselves, have provided a positive counterweight and left an inheritance of love, which even if it cannot eliminate the horror of exploitation, nonetheless mitigates it. On this witness we can build, along this path we can proceed farther.

☙ XXIV ☙

DEATH

The night of the cross and the grave

The love of God—God's power—is stronger than the powers of destruction. So this very "going out," this setting out on the path of the Passion, when Jesus steps outside the boundary of the protective walls of the city, is a gesture of victory ... He summons us to dare to accompany him on his path; for where faith and love are, he is there.

Lying on the bare earth

In this moment, I go back in my memory to the unforgettable experience we all underwent with the death and the funeral of the lamented John Paul II. Around his mortal remains, lying on the bare earth, leaders of nations gathered with people from all social classes and especially the young, in an unforgettable embrace of affection and admiration. The entire world looked to him with trust. To many it seemed as if that intense participation, amplified to the confines of the planet by the social communications media, was like a choral request for help addressed to the Pope by modern humanity which, wracked by fear and uncertainty, questions itself about the future.

On the Easter Vigil

Passing from death to life: this, together with the sacrament of baptism, is the real core of the liturgy of this holy night. Passing from death to life: this is the way by which Christ opened the door, the way the celebrations of the Easter festivities invite us to take.

Support in death

One who can offer nothing to mitigate the suffering of humanity but the expectation that that suffering will one day come to an end has no answer to the most crucial of all questions. On the contrary, by such an answer he affirms suffering as something entirely meaningless and thereby confers on it a devastating horror. What humanity needs is a community that supports the individual in death as well as in life and can make his suffering meaningful.

Measure life by eternity

There was a time when death was a forbidden topic in our society. People tried to ignore its existence as much as possible. It was not permitted to disturb or trouble humanity's enlightened existence. But death did not let itself be so easily ignored. For some time now it has been possible to observe a remarkable change: death has actually become a fashionable topic. We can observe, on the one hand, the trivialization of death, which, like all commonplace realities, is regarded as something to be despised. On the other hand, we can observe the increasing number of books that deal with the borderline experiences of those who have reached the threshold of death and who seek, through the medium of such experiences, which seem almost to have penetrated beyond this threshold, to bring light to the impenetrable darkness that surrounds death and so to offer an answer to the most pressing of all questions: whether our life is to be measured in terms of eternity or is ordered solely to the fleeting moment. Upon reflection, many of these descriptions, which relate profound human experiences, may prove acceptable and can provide insights. Many of them will continue to be problematical. What is obvious in all of them is that man cannot relinquish the struggle to learn about eternity, cannot give up.

🍂 XXV 🍂

PRAYER

The essence of prayer

The first form of our thanksgiving is prayer, thanks given to God in the holy sacrifice. However, prayer must be accompanied by listening to the message and setting out in Christ's company.

"Grant us grace"

Throughout history, the innocent have always been mal-treated, condemned, and killed. How many times have we ourselves preferred success to the truth, our reputation to justice? Strengthen the quiet voice of our conscience, your own voice, in our lives . . . Grant us, ever anew, the grace of conversion.

Why Christians should face East in prayer

Judaism and Islam, now as in the past, take it for granted that we should pray toward the central place of revelation, to the God who has revealed himself to us, in the manner and in the place in which he revealed himself. By contrast, in the western world, an abstract way of thinking, which in a certain way is the fruit of Christian influence, has become dominant. God is spiritual, and God is everywhere: does that not mean that prayer is not tied to a particular place or direction? Now we can indeed pray everywhere, and God is accessible to us everywhere. This idea of the universality of God is a consequence of Christian universality, of the Christian's looking up to God above all gods, the God who embraces the cosmos and is more intimate to us than we are to ourselves. But our knowledge of this universality is the fruit of revelation: God has shown himself to us. Only for this reason do we know him, only for this reason can we confidently pray to him everywhere. And precisely for this reason it is appropriate, now as in the past, that we should express in Christian prayer our turning to the God who has revealed himself to us. Just as God assumed a body and entered the time and space of this world, so it is appropriate to prayer—at least to communal liturgical prayer—that our speaking to God should be "incarnational," that it should be Christological, turned through the incarnate Word to the Triune God. The cosmic symbol of the rising sun expresses the universality of God above all particular places and yet maintains the concreteness of Divine Revelation. Our praying is thus inserted into the procession of the nations to God.

Looking together at the Lord

On the other hand, a common turning to the East during the Eucharistic Prayer remains essential. This is not a case of accidentals, but of essentials. Looking at the priest has no importance. What matters is looking together at the Lord. It is not now a question of dialogue, but of common worship, of setting off toward the One who is to come. What corresponds with the reality of what is happening is not the closed circle, but the common movement forward expressed in a common direction for prayer ...

Christian prayer and transcendental meditation

The difference between transcendental meditation and Christian meditation ... is that man divests himself of his own "I"; he unites with the universal essence of the world; therefore, he remains a bit depersonalized. In Christian meditation, on the contrary, I do not lose my personality; I enter a personal relation with the person of Christ. I enter into relation with the "you" of Christ, and in this way this "I" is not lost; it maintains its identity and responsibility. At the same time it opens, enters a more profound unity, which is the unity of love that does not destroy ... Transcendental meditation is impersonal and, in this sense, "de-personalizing." Christian meditation . . . is "personalizing" and opens to a profound union that is born of love and not of the dissolution of the "I."

☙ XXVI ❧

FAITH

"By means of you, God"

As Christians, we don't wish to be seen ourselves, but wish the Lord to be seen through us. It seems to me that this is the real meaning of this text of the Gospel—even if it says "act in such a way that people may see the work of God and may praise God"—not that people may see the Christians but "by means of you, God." Therefore, the person must not appear, but allow God to be seen through his person.

"Dictatorship of relativism"

Having a clear faith, based on the creed of the Church, is often labeled today as a fundamentalism . . . Whereas relativism, which is letting oneself be tossed and "swept along by every wind of teaching," looks like the only attitude acceptable to today's standards. We are moving toward a dictatorship of relativism which does not recognize anything as certain and which has as its highest goal one's own ego and one's own desires.

Knowledge

Faith itself is a way of knowing.

Seeking certainty

"We are moving toward a dictatorship of relativism which does not recognize anything as for certain and which has as its highest goal one's own ego and one's own desires."

The hidden God

[In the Incarnation] God becomes concrete, tangible in history. He approaches men in bodily form. But this very God, who becomes graspable, remains utterly mysterious. The humiliation he himself has chosen . . . is in a new way, so to speak, the cloud of mystery in which he both conceals and reveals himself. For what greater paradox could there be than this, that God is vulnerable and can be killed? The Word which the Incarnate and Crucified One is, always far surpasses all human words . . .

Faith is solid

But the faith is not primarily the matter for intellectual experimentation, it is rather the solid foundation—the hypostasis, as the Letter to the Hebrews (11:1) tells us—on which we can live and die. As science is not hindered by the certainties reached over time, but rather these certainties provide the conditions for its progress, so also the certainties which faith grants to us open up ever new horizons, while the constant circling around itself of experimental reflection ends in boredom.

Adult faith

Being an "adult" means having a faith which does not follow the waves of today's fashions or the latest novelties. A faith which is deeply rooted in friendship with Christ is adult and mature. It is this friendship that opens us up to all that is good and gives us the knowledge to judge true from false, and deceit from truth. We must become mature in this adult faith; we must guide the flock of Christ to this faith. And it is this faith—only faith—which creates unity and takes form in love. On this theme, Saint Paul offers us some beautiful words—in contrast to the continual ups and downs of those who are like infants, tossed about by the waves: (he says) truth comes through love, that is the basic formula of Christian existence. In Christ, truth and love coincide. To the extent that we draw near to Christ, in our own life, truth and love merge. Love without truth would be blind; truth without love would be like "a resounding gong or a clashing cymbal" (1 Cor 13:1).

"I no longer call you slaves . . . I have called you friends" (John 15:15). So many times we feel like, and it is true, we are only useless servants. (cf Luke 17:10). And despite this, the Lord calls us friends, he makes us his friends, he gives us his friendship. The Lord defines friendship in a dual way. There are no secrets among friends: Christ tells us all everything he hears from the Father; he gives us his full trust, and with that, also knowledge. He reveals his face and his heart to us. He shows us his tenderness for us, his passionate love that goes to the madness of the cross. He entrusts us, he gives us power to speak in his name: "this is my body . . . ," "I forgive you . . ." He entrusts us with his body, the Church. He entrusts our weak minds and our weak hands with his truth—the mystery of God the Father, Son and Holy Spirit; the mystery of God who "so loved the world that he gave his only begotten Son" (John 3:16). He made us his friends—and how do we respond?

A person is at the Center

The Christian faith is not a "religion of the book," the Catechism states concisely (n. 108). This is an extremely important affirmation. The faith does not refer simply to a book, which as such would be the sole and final appeal for the believer. At the center of the Christian faith there is not a book, but a person—Jesus Christ, who is himself the living Word of God and who is handed on, so to speak, in the words of Scripture, which in turn can only be rightly understood in life with him, in the living relation with him. And since Christ built and builds up the Church, the People of God, as his living organism, his "body," essential to the relation with him is participation in the pilgrim people, who are the true and proper human author and owner of the Bible, as has been said. If the living Christ is the true and proper standard of the interpretation of the Bible, this means that we rightly understand this book only in the communal, believing, synchronic and diachronic understanding of the whole Church. Outside of this vital context, the Bible is only a more or less heterogeneous literary collection, not the signpost of a journey for our lives. Scripture and tradition cannot be separated. The great theologian of Tübingen, Johann Adam Möhler, illustrated this necessary connection in an unparalleled way in his classic work *"Die Einheit in der Kirche"* (Unity in the Church), whose study I cannot recommend highly enough. The Catechism emphasizes this connection, which includes the interpretive authority of the Church, as the second Letter of Peter specifically states: "First of all you must understand this, that no prophecy of Scripture is a matter of one's own interpretation..." (2 Pt 1:20).

XXVII

HOPE

Bird in flight

To hope is to fly, said Bonaventure: hope demands of us a radical commitment; it asks of us that all our limbs become movement in order to lift off from the pull of the earth's gravity, in order to rise up to the true heights of our being, to God's promise.

True hope

Ideological optimism is an attempt to have death forgotten by continually talking about history striding toward a perfect society. The fact that this is to skirt round what is really important and that people are being soothed with a lie becomes obvious whenever death itself moves into vicinity. The hope of faith, on the other hand, reveals to us the true future beyond death, and it is only in this way that the real instances of progress that do exist become a future for us, for every individual.

The culmination of hopes

All our anxieties are ultimately fear of losing love and of the total isolation that follows from this. Thus all of our hopes are at bottom hope in the great and boundless love: they hope in paradise, the kingdom of God, being with God and like God, sharing his nature (2 Pet. 1:4). All our hopes find their culmination in the one hope: thy kingdom come, thy will be done on earth as it is in heaven. The earth will become heaven. In his will is to be found all our hope. Learning to pray is learning to hope and thus learning to love.

⚜ XXVIII ⚜

LOVE

Only with the heart

Only with the heart can we see Jesus. Only love purifies us and gives us the ability to see. Only love enables us to recognize the God who is love itself.

Understanding

Love seeks understanding. It wishes to know even better the one whom it loves. It "seeks his face" as Augustine never tires of repeating. Love is the desire for intimate knowledge, so that the quest for intelligence can even be an inner requirement of love. Put another way, there is a coherence of love and truth . . . Christian faith can say of itself, I have found love. Yet love for Christ and of one's neighbor for Christ's like, can enjoy stability and consistency only if its deepest motivation is love for the truth . . . Real love for a neighbor also desires to give him the deepest thing man needs, namely, knowledge and truth.

The opposite of indifference

Love is exactly the opposite of indifference to the other person, it cannot admit that the flame of Christ's love be extinguished in the other, that friendship and knowledge of the Lord should fade, lest "the cares of the world and the delight in riches choke the word" (Mt 13:22).

"He who is to come"

John developed in his Gospel a first theology of memory: the memory is not only the mechanical place for the storage of information, like a computer: it is also this, but much more than this. The moment what is conserved encounters the new, the past as well is illuminated, and what was formerly invisible is now discovered and recognizable. It remains the same, and yet it grows. We discover ever more fully the Word in the words, and thus it is always the same revelation, but it unveils itself and opens into its fullness from generation to generation, indeed, newly in every moment of its own life. God has given us in Christ His Son, Himself, His entire Word. He could not have given us more. In this sense revelation is closed. But because this Word is very God and all the words point back to the Word, precisely for this reason it is never only in the past, but always present and future and always at the same time the anchor of our life in eternity as it is the opening to eternity, the guarantee of the true life, which is stronger than death. Thus, Christ is he who came and at the same time he who is to come. For this reason, we believe in the Redeemer who has already come and nevertheless at the same time we await Him: *Maranatha!*

Ignorance of lovers

In his discourse in the *Symposium*, Aristophanes says that lovers do not know what they really want from each other. From the search for what is more than their pleasure, it is obvious that the souls of both are thirsting for something other than amorous pleasure. But the heart cannot express this "other" thing, "it has only a vague perception of what it truly wants and wonders about it as an enigma."

In Christ's face that is so disfigured, there appears the genuine, extreme beauty: the beauty of love that goes "to the very end"; for this reason it is revealed as greater than falsehood and violence. Whoever has perceived this beauty knows that truth, and not falsehood, is the real aspiration of the world. It is not the false that is "true," but indeed, the Truth. It is, as it were, a new trick of what is false to present itself as "truth" and to say to us: over and above me there is basically nothing, stop seeking or even loving the truth; in doing so you are on the wrong track. The icon of the crucified Christ sets us free from this deception that is so widespread today.

True freedom

"Not my will, but your will be done." In this communion of wills our redemption takes place: being friends of Jesus to become friends of God. How much more we love Jesus, how much more we know him, how much more our true freedom grows as well as our joy in being redeemed. Thank you, Jesus, for your friendship!

Slapped in the face

We return to the "two trumpets" of the Bible with which we started, to the paradox of being able to say of Christ: "You are the fairest of the children of men," and: "He had no beauty, no majesty to draw our eyes, no grace to make us delight in him." In the Passion of Christ the Greek aesthetic that deserves admiration for its perceived contact with the Divine but which remained inexpressible for it, in Christ's passion is not removed but overcome. The experience of the beautiful has received new depth and new realism. The One who is the Beauty itself let himself be slapped in the face, spat upon, crowned with thorns; the Shroud of Turin can help us imagine this in a realistic way. However, it imposes a condition: that we let ourselves be wounded by him, and that we believe in the Love who can risk setting aside his external beauty to proclaim, in this way, the truth of the beautiful.

Proof of the authenticity of my love

In my prayer at communion, I must, on the one hand, look totally toward Christ, allowing myself to be transformed by him, even to burn in his enveloping fire. But I must also always keep clearly in mind how he unites me organically with every other communicant—with the one next to me, who I may not like very much; but also with those who are far away, in Asia, Africa, America, or in any other place.

Becoming one with them, I must learn to open myself toward them and to involve myself in their situations.

This is the proof of the authenticity of my love for Christ. If I am united with Christ, I am together with my neighbor, and this unity is not limited to the moment of communion, but only begins here.

XXIX

HOLINESS

The light of life

In them the fruit of Christ's sacrifice becomes visible: the grain of wheat that died did not remain solitary but yields many fruits down the centuries. In them, Christ shows himself as the One who lives on in the present, who continually calls men and women to imitate him and makes them holy: he conforms them to God. Through these persons the

Kingdom of God enters the world, the light of life, which is opposed to the destruction of humankind by the work of the powers of evil.

In today's second reading, we will hear what makes saints holy, what the right path is for us all: "that we should believe in the name of his Son Jesus Christ and love one another" (1 Jn 3:23). Believing and loving go together: communion with Christ leads to love and the shortest way to our neighbor is communion with Christ, who is closer to each one of us than each one of us is to himself.

Bearing good fruit

"I who chose you and appointed you to go and bear fruit that will remain" (John 15:16). It is here that is expressed the dynamic existence of the Christian, the apostle: I chose you to go and bear fruit . . ." We must be inspired by a holy restlessness: restlessness to bring to everyone the gift of faith, of friendship with Christ. In truth, the love and friendship of God was given to us so that it would also be shared with others. We have received the faith to give it to others . . . We must bring a fruit that will remain. All people want to leave a mark which lasts. But what remains? Money does not. Buildings do not, nor books. After a certain amount of time, whether long or short, all these things disappear. The only thing which remains forever is the human soul, the human person created by God for eternity. The fruit which remains then is that which we have sowed in human souls—love, knowledge, a gesture capable of touching the heart, words which open the soul to joy in the Lord. Let us then go to the Lord and pray to him, so that he may help us bear fruit which remains. Only in this way will the earth be changed from a valley of tears to a garden of God.

"Choose God, Choose life!"

To choose God means, according to Deuteronomy: love him, enter into a communion of thought and will with him, trust him, entrust oneself to him, walk in his ways. The liturgy of Thursday following Ash Wednesday unites with the text of Deuteronomy the Gospel of Luke 9:22-25, that is, the foretelling of the passion of Jesus, in which he corrects Peter's false idea of the Messiah and so rejects the temptation of the false choice, the temptation par excellence. The Lord then applies this foretelling regarding his own path and shows us how we can choose life. "Who wishes to save his own life will lose it, but he who loses his own life for my sake will save it. What does it profit a man to gain the whole world, if he loses his own soul" (Luke 9:24). The cross has nothing to do with the negation of life, with the negation of joy and the fullness of being human. On the contrary, it shows us exactly the true form of how one finds life. He who holds on tightly to his life and wants to be the owner of it, he will lose his life. Only losing oneself is the way to find both oneself and life. The more boldly men have dared to lose themselves, to give themselves, the more they have learned to forget themselves, the greater and richer their life has become. If we think of Francis of Assisi, of Teresa of Avila, of Vincent de Paul, of the Cure d'Ars, of Maximilian Kolbe, we see images of true disciples who show us the way of life, because they show us Christ. From them we can learn to choose God, to choose Christ, and thus to choose life.

❦ XXX ❦

ETERNAL LIFE

The judging Fire

Purgatory is not . . . some kind of supra-worldly concentration camp where one is forced to undergo punishment in a more or less arbitrary fashion. Rather it is the inwardly necessary process of transformation in which a person becomes capable of Christ, capable of God, and thus capable of unity with the whole communion of saints. Simply to look at people with any degree of realism at all is to grasp the necessity of such a process. It does not replace grace by works, but allows the former to achieve its full victory precisely as grace. What actually saves is the full assent of faith. But in most of us, that basic option is buried under a great deal of wood, hay, and straw. Only with difficulty can it peer out from behind the latticework of an egoism we are powerless to pull down with our own hands. Man is the recipient of the divine mercy, yet this does not exonerate him from the need to be transformed. Encounter with the Lord *is* this transformation. It is the fire that burns away our dross and re-forms us to be vessels of eternal joy.

God's justice

In the Easter Vigil, the light of God's justice banishes the darkness of sin and death; the stone at the tomb (made of the same material as the stones in the hands of those who, in today's Gospel, seek to kill Christ) is pushed away forever, and human life is given a future which, in going beyond the categories of this world, reveals the true meaning and the true value of earthly realities.

And we who have been baptized, as children of a world which is still to come, in the liturgy of the Easter Vigil, catch a glimpse of that world and breathe the atmosphere of that world, where God's justice will dwell forever.

And then, renewed and transformed by the Mysteries we celebrate, we can walk in this world justly, living—as the Preface for Lent says so beautifully—"in this passing world with our heart set on the world that will never end."

❦ XXXI ❦

TRUE JOY

Let us pray

Let us pray that the Lord enlighten us, give us the faith that builds the world, the faith that makes us find the path of life, true joy. Amen.

The new world

In conclusion, returning again to the letter to the Ephesians, which says with words from Psalm 68 that Christ, ascending into heaven, "gave gifts to men" (Eph 4:8). The victor offers gifts. And these gifts are apostles, prophets, evangelists, pastors, and teachers. Our ministry is a gift of Christ to humankind, to build up his body—the new world. We live out our ministry in this way, as a gift of Christ to humanity! But at this time, above all, we pray with insistence to the Lord, so that after the great gift of Pope John Paul II, he again gives us a pastor according to his own heart, a pastor who guides us to knowledge in Christ, to his love and to true joy. Amen.

United in praise

The Lord is near us in our conscience, in his word, in his personal presence in the Eucharist: this constitutes the dignity of the Christian and is the reason for his joy. We rejoice therefore, and this joy is expressed in praising God. Today we can see how the closeness of the Lord also brings people together and brings them close to each other: it is because we have the same Lord Jesus Christ in Munich and in Rome that we form one single people of God, across all frontiers, united in the call of conscience, united by the word of God, united through communion with Jesus Christ, united in the praise of God, who is our joy and our redemption.

Help us to follow

Lord . . . help us not to ally ourselves with those who look down on the weak and suffering. Help us to acknowledge your face in the lowly and the outcast . . . May we never complain or become discouraged by life's trials. Help us to follow the path of love and, in submitting to its demands, to find true joy.

"The life of man consists in the vision of God"

The design of God does not annul but demands the action of man. Thus the glory of God shines forth in a new and special way in man, created in his image, precisely when man becomes an active collaborator with Providence and, by means of his liberty, enters to bring to perfection the design of God, through his actions. (Cfr. St. Thomas Aquinas, *Summa Theologiae, I-II, Prologus.*) Above all, man is called to promote life, making of his action an expression of that gift of self, a realization of that charity, which shines forth fully in the face of Christ, perfect image of the Father and model for every man.

There remains, however, another expression to meditate on. It is the expression that completes the phrase of St. Irenaeus which was chosen as the title for our Conference: *"Vita autem hominis visio Dei."* (St. Irenaeus.)

But the life of man consists in the vision of God. Yes, because only when man recognizes his true purpose in his relationship with God, only then is his dignity safe, only then is his freedom rightly directed, only then is his action constructive.

The eternal Christmas

What happened at Christmas was the birth of God's Son, something tremendous and beyond our imagination and reason, yet an event that had always been expected and was indeed necessary. What happened was that God entered our world and came among us ... The eternal meaning of the world came so close to us in this event that we can touch him with our hands and see him with our eyes. What John calls the "Word" is, after all, much more than this. In Greek thought of the period, it meant equally "meaning." It would therefore not be wrong to translate the sentence as: The meaning became flesh.

Part Three

THE PONTIFICATE OF BENEDICT XVI

The events of April 2005, from the passing of John Paul II on April 2, to the funeral Mass for him on April 8, to the election of Benedict XVI on April 19 and his inaugural Mass on April 24, riveted the attention of the world.

The hope, the joy and the beauty of the world experienced during these days is reflected in the eloquent and heartfelt words of Benedict XVI's homilies in the days after his election.

The climax was the inauguration Mass homily, where he moved from a reflection on the "internal desert" of the human heart to a reflection of the duties of the mightiest political leaders. In these pages, we let Benedict, once again, speak for himself.

✦ XXXII ✦

FIRST WORDS AS POPE

Dear brothers and sisters,

After our great Pope, John Paul II, the Cardinals have elected me, a simple, humble worker in God's vineyard. I am consoled by the fact that the Lord knows how to work and how to act, even with insufficient tools, and I especially trust in your prayers. In the joy of the resurrected Lord, trustful of his permanent help, we go ahead, sure that God will help. And Mary, his most beloved Mother, stands on our side. Thank you.

✦ XXXIII ✦

FIRST MESSAGE TO THE WORLD

Venerable Brother Cardinals, Dear Brothers and Sisters in Christ, All you men and women of good will,

"Favor and peace be yours in abundance" (1 Pt 1:2)! At this time, side by side in my heart I feel two contrasting emotions. On the one hand, a sense of inadequacy and human apprehension as I face the responsibility for the universal Church, entrusted to me yesterday as Successor of the Apostle Peter in this See of Rome. On the other, I have a lively feeling of profound gratitude to God who, as the liturgy makes us sing, never leaves his flock untended but leads it down the ages under the guidance of those whom he himself has chosen as the Vicars of his Son and has made shepherds of the flock (cf. *Preface of Apostles I*).

Dear friends, this deep gratitude for a gift of divine mercy is uppermost in my heart in spite of all. And I consider it a special grace which my Venerable Predecessor, John Paul II, has obtained for me. I seem to feel his strong hand clasping mine; I seem to see his smiling eyes and hear his words, at this moment addressed specifically to me, "Do not be afraid!"

The death of the Holy Father John Paul II and the days that followed have been an extraordinary period of grace for the Church and for the whole world. Deep sorrow at his departure and the sense of emptiness that it left in everyone have been tempered by the action of the Risen Christ, which was manifested during long days in the unanimous wave of faith, love, and spiritual solidarity that culminated in his solemn funeral Mass.

We can say it: John Paul II's funeral was a truly extraordinary experience in which, in a certain way, we glimpsed the power of God who, through his Church, wants to make a great family of all the peoples by means of the unifying power of Truth and Love (cf. *Lumen Gentium*, n. 1). Conformed to his Master and Lord, John Paul II crowned his long and fruitful Pontificate at the hour of his death, strengthening Christian people in their faith, gathering them around him and making the entire human family feel more closely united.

How can we not feel sustained by this testimony? How can we fail to perceive the encouragement that comes from this event of grace?

Surprising all my expectations, through the votes of the Venerable Father Cardinals, divine Providence has called me to succeed this great Pope. I am thinking back at this moment to what happened in the neighborhood of Caesarea

Philippi some 2,000 years ago. I seem to hear Peter's words: *"You are the Christ . . . , the Son of the living God,"* and the Lord's solemn affirmation: *"You are 'Peter' and on this rock I will build my Church . . . I will entrust to you the keys of the kingdom of heaven"* (cf. Mt 16:15-19).

You are Christ! You are Peter! I seem to be reliving the same Gospel scene; I, the Successor of Peter, repeat with trepidation the anxious words of the fisherman of Galilee and listen once again with deep emotion to the reassuring promise of the divine Master. Although the weight of responsibility laid on my own poor shoulders is enormous, there is no doubt that the divine power on which I can count is boundless: *"You are 'Peter,' and on this rock I will build my Church"* (Mt 16:18). In choosing me as Bishop of Rome, the Lord wanted me to be his Vicar; he wanted me to be the "rock" on which we can all safely stand. I ask him to compensate for my limitations so that I may be a courageous and faithful Pastor of his flock, ever docile to the promptings of his Spirit.

I am preparing to undertake this special ministry, the "Petrine" ministry at the service of the universal Church, with humble abandonment into the hands of God's Providence. I first of all renew my total and confident loyalty to Christ: *"In Te, Domine, speravi; non confundar in aeternum!"*

Your Eminences, with heartfelt gratitude for the trust you have shown me, I ask you to support me with your prayers and with your constant, active, and wise collaboration. I also ask all my Brothers in the Episcopate to be close to me with their prayers and advice, so that I may truly be the *Servus servorum Dei*. Just as the Lord willed that Peter and the other Apostles make up the one Apostolic College, in the same way the successor of Peter and the Bishops, suc-

cessors of the Apostles—the Council has forcefully re-
asserted this (cf. *Lumen Gentium*, n. 22)—must be closely
united with one another. This collegial communion, despite
the diversity of roles and functions of the Roman Pontiff
and the Bishops, is at the service of the Church and of
unity in the faith, on which the efficacy of evangelizing action in the contemporary world largely depends. Therefore,
it is on this path, taken by my Venerable Predecessors, that
I also intend to set out, with the sole concern of proclaiming the living presence of Christ to the whole world.

I have before my eyes in particular the testimony of Pope
John Paul II. He leaves a Church that is more courageous,
freer, more youthful. She is a Church which, in accordance
with his teaching and example, looks serenely at the past
and is not afraid of the future. With the Great Jubilee she
entered the new millennium, bearing the Gospel, applied to
today's world through the authoritative rereading of the
Second Vatican Council. Pope John Paul II rightly pointed
out the Council as a "compass" by which to take our bear-
ings in the vast ocean of the third millennium (cf. Apostolic
Letter, *Novo Millennio Ineunte*, nn. 57-58). Also, in his spiritual
Testament he noted, "I am convinced that it will long be
granted to the new generations to draw from the treasures
that this 20th-century Council has lavished upon us"
(March 17, 2000; *L'Osservatore Romano* English edition, April
13, 2005, p. 4.).

Thus, as I prepare myself for the service that is proper
to the Successor of Peter, I also wish to confirm my determination to continue to put the Second Vatican Council
into practice, following in the footsteps of my Predecessors
and in faithful continuity with the 2,000-year tradition of
the Church. This very year marks the 40th anniversary of

the conclusion of the Council (December 8, 1965). As the years have passed, the Conciliar Documents have lost none of their timeliness; indeed, their teachings are proving particularly relevant to the new situation of the Church and the current globalized society.

My Pontificate begins in a particularly meaningful way as the Church is living the special Year dedicated to the Eucharist. How could I fail to see this providential coincidence as an element that must mark the ministry to which I am called? The Eucharist, the heart of Christian life and the source of the Church's evangelizing mission, cannot but constitute the permanent center and source of the Petrine ministry that has been entrusted to me.

The Eucharist makes constantly present the Risen Christ who continues to give himself to us, calling us to participate in the banquet of his Body and his Blood. From full communion with him flows every other element of the Church's life: first of all, communion among all the faithful, the commitment to proclaiming and witnessing to the Gospel, the ardor of love for all, especially the poorest and lowliest.

This year, therefore, the Solemnity of *Corpus Christi* must be celebrated with special solemnity. Subsequently, the Eucharist will be the center of the World Youth Day in Cologne in August, and in October, also of the Ordinary Assembly of the Synod of Bishops, whose theme will be: *"The Eucharist, source and summit of the life and mission of the Church."* I ask everyone in the coming months to intensify love and devotion for Jesus in the Eucharist, and to express courageously and clearly faith in the Real Presence of the Lord, especially by the solemnity and the correctness of the celebrations.

I ask this especially of priests, whom I am thinking of with deep affection at this moment. The ministerial Priesthood was born at the Last Supper, together with the Eucharist, as my Venerable Predecessor John Paul II so frequently emphasized. "All the more then must the life of a priest be 'shaped' by the Eucharist" [*Letter to Priests for Holy Thursday 2005*, n. 1, March 23, p. 4]. In the first place, the devout, daily celebration of Holy Mass, the center of the life and mission of every priest, contributes to this goal.

Nourished and sustained by the Eucharist, Catholics cannot but feel encouraged to strive for the full unity for which Christ expressed so ardent a hope in the Upper Room. The Successor of Peter knows that he must make himself especially responsible for his Divine Master's supreme aspiration. Indeed, he is entrusted with the task of strengthening his brethren (cf. Lk 22:32).

With full awareness, therefore, at the beginning of his ministry in the Church of Rome which Peter bathed in his blood, Peter's current Successor takes on as his primary task the duty to work tirelessly to rebuild the full and visible unity of all Christ's followers. This is his ambition, his impelling duty. He is aware that good intentions do not suffice for this. Concrete gestures that enter hearts and stir consciences are essential, inspiring in everyone that inner conversion that is the prerequisite for all ecumenical progress.

Theological dialogue is necessary; the investigation of the historical reasons for the decisions made in the past is also indispensable. But what is most urgently needed is that "purification of memory," so often recalled by John Paul II, which alone can dispose souls to accept the full truth of Christ. Each one of us must come before him, the supreme

Judge of every living person, and render an account to him of all we have done or have failed to do to further the great good of the full and visible unity of all his disciples.

The current Successor of Peter is allowing himself to be called in the first person by this requirement and is prepared to do everything in his power to promote the fundamental cause of ecumenism. Following the example of his Predecessors, he is fully determined to encourage every initiative that seems appropriate for promoting contacts and understanding with the representatives of the different Churches and Ecclesial Communities. Indeed, on this occasion he sends them his most cordial greeting in Christ, the one Lord of us all.

I am thinking back at this time to the unforgettable experience seen by all of us on the occasion of the death and funeral of the late John Paul II. The heads of nations, people from every social class and especially young people gathered round his mortal remains, laid on the bare ground, in an unforgettable embrace of love and admiration. The whole world looked to him with trust. To many it seemed that this intense participation, amplified by the media to reach the very ends of the planet, was like a unanimous appeal for help addressed to the Pope by today's humanity which, upset by uncertainties and fears, was questioning itself on its future.

The Church of today must revive her awareness of the duty to repropose to the world the voice of the One who said: *"I am the light of the world. No follower of mine shall ever walk in darkness; no, he shall possess the light of life"* (Jn 8:12). In carrying out his ministry, the new Pope knows that his task is to make Christ's light shine out before the men and women of today: not his own light, but Christ's.

Aware of this I address everyone, including the followers of other religions or those who are simply seeking an answer to the fundamental questions of life and have not yet found it. I address all with simplicity and affection, to assure them that the Church wants to continue to weave an open and sincere dialogue with them, in the search for the true good of the human being and of society.

I ask God for unity and peace for the human family, and declare the willingness of all Catholics to cooperate for an authentic social development, respectful of the dignity of every human being.

I will make every conscientious effort to continue the promising dialogue initiated by my Venerable Predecessors with the different civilizations, so that mutual understanding may create the conditions for a better future for all.

I am thinking in particular of the young. I offer my affectionate embrace to them, the privileged partners in dialogue with Pope John Paul II, hoping, please God, to meet them in Cologne on the occasion of the upcoming World Youth Day. I will continue our dialogue, dear young people, the future and hope of the Church and of humanity, listening to your expectations in the desire to help you encounter in ever greater depth the living Christ, eternally young.

Mane nobiscum, Domine! Stay with us, Lord! This invocation, which is the principal topic of the Apostolic Letter of John Paul II for the Year of the Eucharist, is the prayer that wells up spontaneously from my heart as I prepare to begin the ministry to which Christ has called me. Like Peter, I too renew to him my unconditional promise of fidelity. I intend to serve him alone, dedicating myself totally to the service of his Church.

To support me in my promise, I call on the motherly intercession of Mary Most Holy, in whose hands I place the present and future of the Church and of myself. May the Holy Apostles Peter and Paul, and all the Saints also intercede for us.

With these sentiments I impart to you, Venerable Brother Cardinals, to those who are taking part in this rite and to all who are watching it on television and listening to it on the radio, a special, affectionate Blessing.

❧ XXXIV ❧

FIRST HOMILY AS POPE

Your Eminences, My dear Brother Bishops and Priests, Distinguished Authorities and Members of the Diplomatic Corps, Dear Brothers and Sisters,

During these days of great intensity, we have chanted the litany of the saints on three different occasions: at the funeral of our Holy Father John Paul II; as the Cardinals entered the Conclave; and again today, when we sang it with the response: *Tu illum adiuva*—sustain the new Successor of Saint Peter.

On each occasion, in a particular way, I found great consolation in listening to this prayerful chant. How alone we all felt after the passing of John Paul II—the Pope who for over 26 years had been our shepherd and guide on our journey through life!

He crossed the threshold of the next life, entering into the mystery of God. But he did not take this step alone. Those who believe are never alone—neither in life nor in death. At that moment, we could call upon the Saints from every age—his friends, his brothers and sisters in the faith—knowing that they would form a living procession to accompany him into the next world, into the glory of God.

We knew that his arrival was awaited. Now we know that he is among his own and is truly at home.

We were also consoled as we made our solemn entrance into Conclave, to elect the one whom the Lord had chosen. How would we be able to discern his name? How could 115 cardinals, from every culture and every country, discover the one on whom the Lord wished to confer the mission of binding and loosing?

Once again, we knew that we were not alone, we knew that we were surrounded, led, and guided by the friends of God. And now, at this moment, weak servant of God that I am, I must assume this enormous task, which truly exceeds all human capacity. How can I do this? How will I be able to do it?

All of you, my dear friends, have just invoked the entire host of Saints, represented by some of the great names in the history of God's dealings with mankind. In this way, I too can say with renewed conviction: I am not alone. I do not have to carry alone what in truth I could never carry alone.

All the Saints of God are there to protect me, to sustain me, and to carry me. And your prayers, my dear friends, your indulgence, your love, your faith, and your hope accompany me. Indeed, the communion of Saints consists not only of the great men and women who went before us and whose names we know. All of us belong to the communion of Saints, we who have been baptized in the name of the Father, and of the Son, and of the Holy Spirit, we who draw life from the gift of Christ's Body and Blood, through which he transforms us and makes us like himself.

Yes, the Church is alive—this is the wonderful experience of these days. During those sad days of the Pope's illness and death, it became wonderfully evident to us that the Church is alive. And the Church is young. She holds within herself the future of the world and therefore shows each of us the way towards the future. The Church is alive and we are seeing it: we are experiencing the joy that the Risen Lord promised his followers. The Church is alive—she is alive because Christ is alive, because he is truly risen.

In the suffering that we saw on the Holy Father's face in those days of Easter, we contemplated the mystery of Christ's Passion and we touched his wounds. But throughout these days we have also been able, in a profound sense, to touch the Risen One. We have been able to experience the joy that he promised, after a brief period of darkness, as the fruit of his resurrection.

The Church is alive—with these words, I greet with great joy and gratitude all of you gathered here, my venerable brother Cardinals and bishops, my dear priests, deacons, Church workers, catechists.

I greet you, men and women religious, witnesses of the transfiguring presence of God. I greet you, members of the lay faithful, immersed in the great task of building up the Kingdom of God which spreads throughout the world, in every area of life. With great affection I also greet all those who have been reborn in the sacrament of Baptism but are not yet in full communion with us; and you, my brothers and sisters of the Jewish people, to whom we are joined by a great shared spiritual heritage, one rooted in God's irrevocable promises. Finally, like a wave gathering force, my thoughts go out to all men and women of today, to believers and non-believers alike.

Dear friends! At this moment there is no need for me to present a program of governance. I was able to give an indication of what I see as my task in my Message of Wednesday, April 20, and there will be other opportunities to do so.

My real program of governance is not to do my own will, not to pursue my own ideas, but to listen, together with the whole Church, to the word and the will of the Lord, to be guided by Him, so that He himself will lead the Church at this hour of our history.

Instead of putting forward a program, I should simply like to comment on the two liturgical symbols which represent the inauguration of the Petrine ministry; both these symbols, moreover, reflect clearly what we heard proclaimed in today's readings.

The first symbol is the pallium, woven in pure wool, which will be placed on my shoulders. This ancient sign, which the Bishops of Rome have worn since the fourth century, may be considered an image of the yoke of Christ, which the bishop of this City, the servant of the servants of God, takes upon his shoulders.

God's yoke is God's will, which we accept. And this will does not weigh down on us, oppressing us and taking away our freedom. To know what God wants, to know where the path of life is found—this was Israel's joy, this was her great privilege.

It is also our joy: God's will does not alienate us, it purifies us—even if this can be painful—and so it leads us to ourselves. In this way, we serve not only him, but the salvation of the whole world, of all history.

The symbolism of the pallium is even more concrete: the lamb's wool is meant to represent the lost, sick, or weak sheep which the shepherd places on his shoulders and carries to the waters of life.

For the Fathers of the Church, the parable of the lost sheep, which the shepherd seeks in the desert, was an image of the mystery of Christ and the Church. The human race—every one of us—is the sheep lost in the desert which no longer knows the way.

The Son of God will not let this happen; he cannot abandon humanity in so wretched a condition. He leaps to his feet and abandons the glory of heaven, in order to go in search of the sheep and pursue it, all the way to the Cross.

He takes it upon his shoulders and carries our humanity; he carries us all—he is the good shepherd who lays down his life for the sheep.

What the pallium indicates first and foremost is that we are all carried by Christ. But at the same time it invites us to carry one another. Hence the pallium becomes a symbol of the shepherd's mission, of which the Second Reading and the Gospel speak.

The pastor must be inspired by Christ's holy zeal: for him it is not a matter of indifference that so many people are living in the desert.

And there are so many kinds of desert. There is the desert of poverty, the desert of hunger and thirst, the desert of abandonment, of loneliness, of destroyed love.

There is the desert of God's darkness, the emptiness of souls no longer aware of their dignity or the goal of human life. The external deserts in the world are growing, because the internal deserts have become so vast.

Therefore the earth's treasures no longer serve to build God's garden for all to live in, but they have been made to serve the powers of exploitation and destruction.

The Church as a whole and all her pastors, like Christ, must set out to lead people out of the desert, towards the place of life, towards friendship with the Son of God, towards the One who gives us life, and life in abundance.

The symbol of the lamb also has a deeper meaning. In the ancient near East, it was customary for kings to style themselves shepherds of their people. This was an image of their power, a cynical image: to them their subjects were like sheep, which the shepherd could dispose of as he wished.

When the shepherd of all humanity, the living God, himself became a lamb, he stood on the side of the lambs, with those who are downtrodden and killed. This is how he reveals himself to be the true shepherd: "I am the Good Shepherd . . . I lay down my life for the sheep," Jesus says of himself (Jn 10:14).

It is not power, but love that redeems us! This is God's sign: he himself is love. How often we wish that God would show himself stronger, that he would strike decisively, defeating evil and creating a better world.

All ideologies of power justify themselves in exactly this way, they justify the destruction of whatever would stand in the way of progress and the liberation of humanity. We suffer on account of God's patience.

And yet, we need his patience. God, who became a lamb, tells us that the world is saved by the Crucified One, not by those who crucified him. The world is redeemed by the patience of God. It is destroyed by the impatience of man.

One of the basic characteristics of a shepherd must be to love the people entrusted to him, even as he loves Christ whom he serves. "Feed my sheep," says Christ to Peter, and now, at this moment, he says it to me as well. Feeding means loving, and loving also means being ready to suffer.

Loving means giving the sheep what is truly good, the nourishment of God's truth, of God's word, the nourishment of his presence, which he gives us in the Blessed Sacrament.

My dear friends—at this moment I can only say: pray for me, that I may learn to love the Lord more and more.

Pray for me, that I may learn to love his flock more and more—in other words, you, the holy Church, each one of you and all of you together. Pray for me, that I may not flee for fear of the wolves. Let us pray for one another, that the Lord will carry us and that we will learn to carry one another.

The second symbol used in today's liturgy to express the inauguration of the Petrine Ministry is the presentation of the fisherman's ring.

Peter's call to be a shepherd, which we heard in the Gospel, comes after the account of a miraculous catch of fish: after a night in which the disciples had let down their nets without success, they see the Risen Lord on the shore. He tells them to let down their nets once more, and the nets become so full that they can hardly pull them in; 153 large fish: "and although there were so many, the net was not torn" (Jn 21:11).

This account, coming at the end of Jesus's earthly journey with his disciples, corresponds to an account found at the beginning: there too, the disciples had caught nothing the entire night; there too, Jesus had invited Simon once more to put out into the deep.

And Simon, who was not yet called Peter, gave the wonderful reply: "Master, at your word I will let down the nets." And then came the conferral of his mission: "Do not be afraid. Henceforth you will be catching men" (Lk 5:1-11).

Today too the Church and the successors of the Apostles are told to put out into the deep sea of history and to let down the nets, so as to win men and women over to the Gospel—to God, to Christ, to true life.

The Fathers made a very significant commentary on this singular task. This is what they say: for a fish, created for water, it is fatal to be taken out of the sea, to be removed from its vital element to serve as human food.

But in the mission of a fisher of men, the reverse is true. We are living in alienation, in the salt waters of suffering and death; in a sea of darkness without light.

The net of the Gospel pulls us out of the waters of death and brings us into the splendor of God's light, into true life. It is really true: as we follow Christ in this mission to be fishers of men, we must bring men and women out of the sea that is salted with so many forms of alienation and onto the land of life, into the light of God.

It is really so: the purpose of our lives is to reveal God to men. And only where God is seen does life truly begin. Only when we meet the living God in Christ do we know what life is. We are not some casual and meaningless product of evolution.

Each of us is the result of a thought of God. Each of us is willed, each of us is loved, each of us is necessary. There is nothing more beautiful than to be surprised by the

Gospel, by the encounter with Christ. There is nothing more beautiful than to know Him and to speak to others of our friendship with Him.

The task of the shepherd, the task of the fisher of men, can often seem wearisome. But it is beautiful and wonderful, because it is truly a service to joy, to God's joy which longs to break into the world.

Here I want to add something: both the image of the shepherd and that of the fisherman issue an explicit call to unity. "I have other sheep that are not of this fold; I must lead them too, and they will heed my voice. So there shall be one flock, one shepherd" (Jn 10:16); these are the words of Jesus at the end of his discourse on the Good Shepherd.

And the account of the 153 large fish ends with the joyful statement: "although there were so many, the net was not torn" (Jn 21:11). Alas, beloved Lord, with sorrow we must now acknowledge that it has been torn! But no—we must not be sad! Let us rejoice because of your promise, which does not disappoint, and let us do all we can to pursue the path towards the unity you have promised. Let us remember it in our prayer to the Lord, as we plead with him: yes, Lord, remember your promise. Grant that we may be one flock and one shepherd! Do not allow your net to be torn, help us to be servants of unity!

At this point, my mind goes back to October 22, 1978, when Pope John Paul II began his ministry here in Saint Peter's Square. His words on that occasion constantly echo in my ears: "Do not be afraid! Open wide the doors for Christ!"

The pope was addressing the mighty, the powerful of this world, who feared that Christ might take away something of their power if they were to let him in, if they were to allow the faith to be free.

Yes, he would certainly have taken something away from them: the dominion of corruption, the manipulation of law and the freedom to do as they pleased. But he would not have taken away anything that pertains to human freedom or dignity, or to the building of a just society.

The pope was also speaking to everyone, especially the young. Are we not perhaps all afraid in some way? If we let Christ enter fully into our lives, if we open ourselves totally to him, are we not afraid that He might take something away from us?

Are we not perhaps afraid to give up something significant, something unique, something that makes life so beautiful? Do we not then risk ending up diminished and deprived of our freedom?

And once again the Pope said: No! If we let Christ into our lives, we lose nothing, nothing, absolutely nothing of what makes life free, beautiful and great.

No! Only in this friendship are the doors of life opened wide. Only in this friendship is the great potential of human existence truly revealed. Only in this friendship do we experience beauty and liberation.

And so, today, with great strength and great conviction, on the basis of long personal experience of life, I say to you, dear young people: Do not be afraid of Christ! He takes nothing away, and he gives you everything. When we give ourselves to him, we receive a hundredfold in return.

Yes, open, open wide the doors to Christ—and you will find true life. Amen.

ACKNOWLEDGMENTS

I would like to acknowledge the help of a number of family members, friends, and colleagues, whose advice and support helped me to prepare this small volume on Pope Benedict XVI. My colleagues at "Inside the Vatican" were unfailingly supportive: Delia Gallagher, Shena Muldoon, John Mallon, Lucy Gordan, Micaela Biferali, Giuseppe Sabatelli, Alberto Carosa, Grzegorz Galazka, Thierry Cagianut, Hugh Pimentel, Dennis Musk, and Leonid Sevastianov. The American theologian Anthony Valle and his wife Marta Valle, whose wedding Mass was celebrated by Cardinal Ratzinger last year, provided key insights and typed numerous passages. The German journalist Paul Badde and his daughter, Christina Badde, assisted me throughout the project, during an April in Rome when the city was crowded with millions of pilgrims and historic events occurred daily. Without the help of Paul and Christina, I would not have been able to complete this volume in just two weeks. My editor at Doubleday, Trace Murphy, was ever efficient, patient, and precise. And my whole family was wonderfully supportive, from my parents, William and Ruth Moynihan, who made many valuable suggestions daily via phone and email, to my wife, Priscilla, who carried on family life as the book took shape, and to my beloved sons Christopher and Luke, who did their homework while I burned the midnight oil. Thanks to all of you.

NOTES

The sources for all the statements by Pope Benedict XVI quoted earlier in this book are listed below. The great majority of these were written or spoken when the Pope was Joseph Cardinal Ratzinger. His name is given initially but it is not repeated for each entry. Except for official Vatican publications the material that originally appeared in Italian has been translated by the editor of this volume

pg. 83 December 10, 2000, Ratzinger, in Rome on "The New Evangelization" to participants in the Jubilee for Catechists.

Joseph Ratzinger, *The Nature and Mission of Theology,* Ignatius, 1995, p. 25.

December 10, 2000, Ratzinger, in Rome on "The New Evangelization" to participants in the Jubilee for Catechists.

pg. 84 December 10, 2000, Ratzinger, in Rome on "The New Evangelization" to participants in the Jubilee for Catechists.

December 10, 2000, Ratzinger, in Rome on "The New Evangelization" to participants in the Jubilee for Catechists.

pg. 85   December 10, 2000, Ratzinger, in Rome on "The New
         Evangelization" to participants in the Jubilee for
         Catechists.

         December 10, 2000, Ratzinger, in Rome on "The New
         Evangelization" to participants in the Jubilee for
         Catechists.

         December 10, 2000, Ratzinger, in Rome on "The New
         Evangelization" to participants in the Jubilee for
         Catechists.

pg. 86   December 10, 2000, Ratzinger, in Rome on "The New
         Evangelization" to participants in the Jubilee for
         Catechists.

         December 10, 2000, Ratzinger, in Rome on "The New
         Evangelization" to participants in the Jubilee for
         Catechists.

pg. 87   December 10, 2000, Ratzinger, in Rome on "The New
         Evangelization" to participants in the Jubilee for
         Catechists.

         December 10, 2000, Ratzinger, in Rome on "The New
         Evangelization" to participants in the Jubilee for
         Catechists.

pg. 88   December 10, 2000, Ratzinger, in Rome on "The New
         Evangelization" to participants in the Jubilee for
         Catechists.

         The Sabbath of History, 1998.

         Salt of the Earth, p. 22

         December 10, 2000, Ratzinger, in Rome on "The New
         Evangelization" to participants in the Jubilee for
         Catechists.

pg. 89   December 10, 2000, Ratzinger, in Rome on "The New
         Evangelization" to participants in the Jubilee for
         Catechists.

Interview with Antonella Palermo of Vatican Radio in
2001, published by *Zenit*, April 27, 2005.

On June 2, 2002, the Cardinal delivered a far-ranging
and detailed Eucharistic instruction to the 1st diocesan Eucharistic Congress in Benevento, Italy, south
of Rome. Entitled "Eucharist, Communion and Solidarity"—translated from the Italian by Robert
Moynihan, published in *Inside the Vatican* in the issue
of August-September, 2002.

pg. 90   Joseph Ratzinger, *The Nature and Mission of Theology*, Ignatius, 1995, p. 24.

Salt of the Earth p. 112.

pg. 91   *God and the World*, Peter Seewald, Ignatius, 2002, p. 18.

Ratzinger, "Choose Life," May 1997, *Inside the Vatican* (my
own translation), Lenten talk given March 5, 1997, in
Rome at the Basilica of St. John Lateran.

pg. 92   *God and the World*, Peter Seewald, Ignatius, 2002, p. 19.

Ratzinger, "Choose Life," May 1997, *Inside the Vatican* (my
own translation), Lenten talk given March 5, 1997, in
Rome at the Basilica of St. John Lateran.

God and the World, Peter Seewald, Ignatius, 2002, p. 21.

June 2, 2002, the Cardinal delivered a far-ranging and
detailed Eucharistic instruction to the 1st diocesan
Eucharistic Congress in Benevento, Italy, south of
Rome. Entitled "Eucharist, Communion and Solidarity."

pg. 93   *Behold the Pierced One*, p. 69.

pg. 94   Declaration *Dominus Iesus:* On the Unicity and Salvific
Universality of Jesus Christ and the Church.

Cardinal Joseph Ratzinger, Saturday, October, 18, 2003,
L'Osservatore Romano, Weekly Edition in English, November 12, 2003, p. 10.

Behold the Pierced One, p. 69.

Ratzinger, "Choose Life," May 1997, *Inside the Vatican* (my own translation), Lenten talk given March 5, 1997, in Rome at the Basilica of St. John Lateran.

pg. 95   *Salt of the Earth,* p. 20.

Journey Towards Easter, p. 35.

pg. 96   Funeral Mass for Fr. Luigi Giussani, Milan Cathedral, February 24, 2005.

40th Anniversary of *Gaudium et Spes,* St. Peter's Basilica.

pg. 97   40th Anniversary of *Gaudium et Spes,* St. Peter's Basilica.

"The Feeling of Things, the Contemplation of Beauty" Meeting at Rimini (August 24–30, 2002).

pg. 98   Ratzinger, "Choose Life," May 1997, *Inside the Vatican* (my own translation), Lenten talk given March 5, 1997, in Rome at the Basilica of St. John Lateran.

pg. 99   Way of the Cross at the Colosseum, Good Friday 2005, Meditations and Prayers.

Way of the Cross at the Colosseum, Good Friday 2005, Meditations and Prayers.

Interview, Cardinal Ratzinger Calls Relativism the New Face of Intolerance, Has Advice for Young Theologians; Speaks of the Role of Universities, Murcia, Spain, Dec. 1, 2002 (Zenit.org).

pg. 100   *Introduction to Christianity,* p. 256.

pg. 101   *Introduction to Christianity,* p. 257.

Joseph Ratzinger, Comment on the Message of Fatima, June 26, 2000.

Ratzinger, "Choose Life," May 1997, *Inside the Vatican* (my own translation), Lenten talk given March 5, 1997, in Rome at the Basilica of St. John Lateran.

Ratzinger Report, p. 151.

pg. 102   [*Seek That Which Is Above. Meditations through the Year,* Ignatius

Press, San Francisco 1986, translated by Graham
Harrison, pp. 101–102.]

[*Seek That Which Is Above. Meditations through the Year,* Ignatius
Press, San Francisco 1986, translated by Graham
Harrison, pp. 102–103.]

Ratzinger, Comment on the Secret of Fatima, June 26,
2000.

pg. 103   *Introduction to Christianity,* p. 213.

Way of the Cross at the Colosseum, Good Friday 2005,
Meditations and Prayers.

Ratzinger Report, p. 106.

Way of the Cross at the Colosseum, Good Friday 2005,
Meditations and Prayers.

pg. 104   *In the Beginning . . . A Catholic Understanding of the Story of
Creation and the Fall,* William B. Eerdmans Publishing
Company, Grand Rapids (Michigan) 1995, translated
by Boniface Ramsey, pp. 98–99.

*In the Beginning . . . A Catholic Understanding of the Story of
Creation and the Fall,* William B. Eerdmans Publishing
Company, Grand Rapids (Michigan) 1995, translated
by Boniface Ramsey, pp. 44–46.

pg. 105   Interview with Antonella Palermo of Vatican Radio in
2001, published by *Zenit,* April 27, 2005.

Ratzinger, lecture released by the Vatican Press Office
on November 24, 1994, printed in *Inside the Vatican,*
January, 1995, my own translation.

pg. 106   *In the Beginning . . . A Catholic Understanding of the Story of
Creation and the Fall,* William B. Eerdmans Publishing
Company, Grand Rapids (Michigan) 1995, translated
by Boniface Ramsey, p. 49.

Way of the Cross at the Colosseum, Good Friday 2005,
Meditations and Prayers.

Ordinariatskorrespondenz, December 25, 1979.

pg. 107 *Dogma und Verkundigung*, pp. 397-98.

Way of the Cross, Meditations and Prayers, Good Friday 2005.

Ratzinger, "Choose Life," May 1997, *Inside the Vatican* (my own translation), Lenten talk given March 5, 1997, in Rome at the Basilica of St. John Lateran.

pg. 109 Address to Rabbis on February 2, 1984, in Jerusalem.

EWTN Interview with Raymond Arroyo, September 5, 2003.

pg. 110 Homily for the Easter Vigil Mass, Altar of the Confession in St. Peter's Basilica, Holy Saturday, March 26, 2005.

Diener eurer Freude, pp. 108–9.

pg. 111 Ratzinger, "Choose Life," May 1997, *Inside the Vatican* (my own translation), Lenten talk given March 5, 1997, in Rome at the Basilica of St. John Lateran.

Pope Benedict XVI at the end of Mass with the College of Cardinals assembled in the Sistine Chapel on April 20, 2005, the day after his election. It outlines the program for his pontificate.

pg. 112 Pope Benedict XVI at the end of Mass with the College of Cardinals assembled in the Sistine Chapel on April 20, 2005, the day after his election. It outlines the program for his pontificate.

pg. 113 Homily for the Easter Vigil Mass, Altar of the Confession in St. Peter's Basilica, Holy Saturday, March 26, 2005.

Homily, Mass of Easter Vigil 2005.

Presentation of the Apostolic Letter in the Form of *Motu Proprio Misericordia Dei Intervention*, Thursday, May 2, 2002.

pg. 114   Homily of Commemoration Mass in Honor of the Popes Paul VI and John Paul I, Altar of the Chair, St. Peter's Basilica, September 28, 2004.

June 2, 2002, the Cardinal delivered a far-ranging and detailed Eucharistic instruction to the 1st diocesan Eucharistic Congress in Benevento, Italy, south of Rome. Entitled "Eucharist, Communion and Solidarity."

Pope Benedict XVI at the end of Mass with the College of Cardinals assembled in the Sistine Chapel on April 20, 2005, the day after his election. It outlines the program for his pontificate.

pg. 115   Lecture at the bishops' conference of the region of Campania in Benevento (Italy) on the topic: "Eucharist, Communion and Solidarity."

pg. 116   June 2, 2002, the Cardinal delivered a far-ranging and detailed Eucharistic instruction to the 1st diocesan Eucharistic Congress in Benevento, Italy, south of Rome. Entitled "Eucharist, Communion and Solidarity."

Congregation for The Doctrine of the Faith, Address of Cardinal Joseph Ratzinger October 9, 2002, Current Doctrinal Relevance of the Catechism of the Catholic Church, The Catechism of the Catholic Church: Ten years since its publication (October 11, 1992).

pg. 117   *My Life: Recollections 1927–1977*, 1996.

pg. 118   *Seeking God's Face*, p. 30.

Pope Benedict XVI at the end of Mass with the College of Cardinals assembled in the Sistine Chapel on April 20, 2005, the day after his election. It outlines the program for his pontificate.

pg. 123   Ratzinger, lecture released by the Vatican Press Office
          on November 24, 1994, printed in *Inside the Vatican,*
          January 1995, my own translation.

          Presentation of encyclical *Veritatis Splendor,* November
          1993.

          Ratzinger Report, p. 83.

pg. 124   Presentation of encyclical *Veritatis Splendor,* November
          1993.

          "The Heart of Europe," on the book *Values in Times of
          Upheaval* published by Munich's *Sueddeutsche Zeitung* on
          Wednesday, April 13, 2005.

pg. 125   *Seek That Which Is Above,* p. 158.

          Homily on the 40th Anniversary of *Gaudium et Spes,* St.
          Peter's Basilica, Friday, March 18, 2005.

pg. 126   June 2, 2002, the Cardinal delivered a far-ranging and
          detailed Eucharistic instruction to the 1st diocesan
          Eucharistic Congress in Benevento, Italy, south of
          Rome, entitled "Eucharist, Communion and Solidar-
          ity."

          Homily on the 40th Anniversary of *Gaudium et Spes,* St.
          Peter's Basilica, March 18, 2005.

pg. 127   Homily on the 40th Anniversary of *Gaudium et Spes,* St.
          Peter's Basilica, March 18, 2005.

          Commemoration Mass in Honor of the Popes Paul VI
          and John Paul I, Altar of the Chair, St. Peter's Basil-
          ica, September 28, 2004.

          Ratzinger, "Choose Life," May 1997, *Inside the Vatican* (my
          own translation), Lenten talk given on March 5,
          1997, in Rome at the Basilica of St. John Lateran.

pg. 128   *Zeitfragen und christlicher Glaube,* p. 63.

          Zeitfragen und christlicher Glaube, pp. 60–61.

pg. 129   Way of the Cross, Good Friday 2005.

Way of the Cross, Good Friday 2005.

"The Heart of Europe," interview with Cardinal Joseph
Ratzinger on his new book *Values in Times of Upheaval*
published by Munich's *Sueddeutsche Zeitung* on Wednesday, April 13, 2005.

pg. 130 Roman homilies, January 29, 1984.

Dogma und Verkundigung, pp. 391–92.

Ratzinger, *Turning Point for Europe*, pp. 175–77.

pg. 131 Ratzinger, *Church Ecumenism and Politics*, p. 163.

"The Heart of Europe," on the book *Values in Times of
Upheaval*" published by Munich's *Sueddeutsche Zeitung* on
Wednesday, April 13, 2005.

pg. 132 *Deutsche Tagespost*, April 9, 1982.

pg. 133 Milan Cathedral, February 24, 2005. Funeral Mass for
Fr. Giussani.

Milan Cathedral, February 24, 2005. Funeral Mass for
Fr. Giussani.

pg. 134 June 2, 2002, the Cardinal delivered a far-ranging and
detailed Eucharistic instruction to the 1st diocesan
Eucharistic Congress in Benevento, Italy, south of
Rome, entitled "Eucharist, Communion and Solidarity."

Art, image and artists, sacred art, inspired by faith, both
reflects and informs the culture, Part II.

pg. 135 The Beauty and the Truth of Christ, CL Meeting in
Rimini: August 24–30; taken from: *L'Osservatore Romano*, Weekly Edition in English, November 6, 2002,
p. 6.

The Beauty and the Truth of Christ, CL Meeting in
Rimini: August 24–30; taken from: *L'Osservatore Romano*, Weekly Edition in English, November 6, 2002,
p. 6.

The Beauty and the Truth of Christ, CL Meeting in
Rimini: August 24–30; taken from: *L'Osservatore Romano*, Weekly Edition in English, November 6, 2002,
p. 6.

pg. 136   25th Anniversary of the Pontificate of John Paul II:
Concert offered by the *Mitteldeutscher Rundfunk* Orchestra, October 17, 2003.

25th Anniversary of the Pontificate of John Paul II:
Concert offered by the *Mitteldeutscher Rundfunk* Orchestra, October 17, 2003.

25th Anniversary of the Pontificate of John Paul II:
Concert offered by the *Mitteldeutscher Rundfunk* Orchestra, October 17, 2003.

pg. 137   Ratzinger, *Commentary, Secret of Fatima*, June 26, 2000.

pg. 138   On June 2, 2002, the Cardinal delivered a far-ranging
and detailed Eucharistic instruction to the 1st
diocesan Eucharistic Congress in Benevento, Italy,
south of Rome, entitled "Eucharist, Communion,
and Solidarity."

Bavarian radio broadcast, October 2, 1977.

pg. 139   Meeting with the representatives of the Christian
churches and ecclesial communities and other world
religions (April 25, 2005).

Cardinal Ratzinger at a press conference in Spain before
the first International Congress of the San Dámaso
Faculty of Theology.

pg. 140   From a conference on Faith, Truth, and Tolerance,
March 2002.

Zur Lage des Glaubens, pp. 164–65.

Inter-religious Dialogue and Jewish-Christian Relations,
Produced for a Session of the Academy of Moral
and Political Sciences, Paris. It first appeared in *Com-*

munio 26, 1997, and was published in *Many Religions, One Covenant.*

pg. 141 Pope Benedict XVI at the end of Mass with the College of Cardinals assembled in the Sistine Chapel on April 20, 2005, the day after his election. It outlines the program for his pontificate.

pg. 142 Pope Benedict XVI at the end of Mass with the College of Cardinals assembled in the Sistine Chapel on April 20, 2005, the day after his election. It outlines the program for his pontificate.

Ratzinger Report, pp. 84.

pg. 143 "The Heart of Europe," on the book *Values in Times of Upheaval* published by Munich's *Sueddeutsche Zeitung* on Wednesday, April 13, 2005.

Homily on the 40th Anniversary of *Gaudium et Spes,* St. Peter's Basilica, March 18, 2005.

Presentation of encyclical *Veritatis Splendor,* November 1993.

pg. 144 *Glaube und Zukunft,* pp. 120–21, 123.

pg. 148 EWTN Interview with Raymond Arroyo, September 5, 2003.

pg. 149 Way of the Cross at the Colosseum, Prayers and Meditations, Good Friday 2005.

pg. 150 *God and the World,* Ignatius.

Way of the Cross at the Colosseum, Prayers and Meditations, Good Friday 2005.

Homily at the Mass for the Election of the Roman Pontiff, April 18, 2005.

pg. 151 *Veraltetes Glaubensbekenutnis,* pp. 105–6.

pg. 152 *To Look on Christ, Exercises in Faith, Hope and Love,* pp. 68–70.

pg. 154 Way of the Cross, Good Friday 2005.

Introduction to Christianity, pp. 196–97.

Worthiness to Receive Holy Communion. General
Principles, Letter to U.S. Bishops, June 2004.

pg. 155 The Beauty and the Truth of Christ, CL Meeting in
Rimini: August 24–30; taken from: *L'Osservatore Romano,* Weekly Edition in English, November 6, 2002,
p. 6.

pg. 156 On June 2, 2002, the Cardinal delivered a far-ranging
and detailed Eucharistic instruction to the 1st
diocesan Eucharistic Congress in Benevento, Italy,
south of Rome. Entitled "Eucharist, Communion,
and Solidarity."

Behold the Pierced One, 1986, p. 108.

First Homily, April 20, 2005.

pg. 157 Homily, Easter Vigil, March 25, 2005.

Bavarian radio broadcast, 1978.

Christlicher Glaube und Europa, pp. 127–38.

pg. 158 25th Anniversary of the Pontificate of John Paul II,
Symposium of the College of Cardinals, October 15,
2003.

pg. 159 Way of the Cross, Good Friday 2005.

Society for the Renewal of the Sacred Liturgy, Vol. VI,
No. 3: May 2000.

pg. 160 Society for the Renewal of the Sacred Liturgy, Vol. VI,
No. 3: May 2000.

Interview: "Cardinal Ratzinger Calls Relativism the
New Face of Intolerance, Has Advice for Young
Theologians; Speaks of the Role of Universities"
Murcia, Spain, December 1, 2002 (Zenit.org).

pg. 161 Conversation with Robert Moynihan.

Mass hours before the beginning of the conclave that
would elect him Pope, April 18, 2005.

Pontifical Biblical Commision, on the 100th anniversary of the Pontifical Biblical Commission, Relationship between Magisterium and exegetes.

pg. 162 Mass hours before the beginning of the conclave that would elect him Pope, April 18, 2005.

Many Religions—One Covenant, Ignatius, 1999, pp. 107–8.

"Current Doctrinal Relevance of the Catechism of the Catholic Church," The Catechism of the Catholic Church: Ten years since its publication (October 11, 1992).

Cardinal Joseph Ratzinger's homily, April 18, 2005.

pg. 164 "Current Doctrinal Relevance of the Catechism of the Catholic Church," The Catechism of the Catholic Church: Ten years since its publication (October 11, 1992.)

pg. 165 *To look on Christ—Exercises in Faith, Hope and Love*, p. 62.

To look on Christ—Exercises in Faith, Hope and Love, p. 49.

To look on Christ—Exercises in Faith, Hope and Love, p. 65.

pg. 166 Way of the Cross, Good Friday 2005.

The Nature and Mission of Theology, Ignatius, 1995, p. 27.

Homily, Commemoration Mass in Honor of the Popes Paul VI and John Paul I, Altar of the Chair, St. Peter's Basilica, September 28, 2004.

Ratzinger, "Choose Life," May 1997, *Inside the Vatican* (my own translation), Lenten talk given March 5, 1997, in Rome at the Basilica of St. John Lateran.

pg. 167 "The Beauty and the Truth of Christ," Cardinal Joseph Ratzinger to CL Meeting in Rimini: August 24–30; taken from: *L'Osservatore Romano*, Weekly Edition in English, November 6, 2002, p. 6.

pg. 168 Homily at the Mass for the Election of the Roman Pontiff, April 18, 2005.

"The Beauty and the Truth of Christ," Cardinal Joseph Ratzinger to CL Meeting in Rimini: August 24–30; taken from: *L'Osservatore Romano*, Weekly Edition in English, November 6, 2002, p. 6.

pg. 169 On June 2, 2002, the Cardinal delivered a far-ranging and detailed Eucharistic instruction to the 1st diocesan Eucharistic Congress in Benevento, Italy, south of Rome. Entitled "Eucharist, Communion, and Solidarity."

Greetings to John Paul II with a Message of Congratulations and Best Wishes on His 83rd Birthday, May 18, 2003.

pg. 170 Homily at the Mass for the Election of the Roman Pontiff, April 18, 2005.

pg. 171 Ratzinger, "Choose Life," May 1997, *Inside the Vatican* (my own translation), Lenten talk given March 5, 1997, in Rome at the Basilica of St. John Lateran.

pg. 172 *Eschatology: Death and Eternal Life*, 1977.

40th Anniversary of *Gaudium et Spes*, Homily of Cardinal Joseph Ratzinger, St. Peter's Basilica, Friday, March 18, 2005.

pg. 173 Milan Cathedral, February 24, 2005. Funeral Mass for Fr. Giussani.

Conclusion of Homily at the Mass for the Election of the Roman Pontiff, April 18, 2005.

pg. 174 *God is Near Us: The Eucharist, the Heart of Life.*

Way of the Cross at the Colosseum, Good Friday 2005, Meditations and Prayers.

Ratzinger, lecture released by the Vatican Press Office on November 24, 1994, printed in *Inside the Vatican*, January, 1995, my own translation.

pg. 175 *Seeking God's Face*, p. 64.